Reminiscences

of

Vice Admiral Felix L. Johnson

U. S. Navy (Retired)

U. S. Naval Institute
Annapolis, Maryland
1974

Preface

This volume contains the transcript of five tape recorded interviews with Vice Admiral Felix L. Johnson, U. S. Navy (Retired). The interviews were obtained by John T. Mason, Jr. for the Oral History program of the U. S. Naval Institute. All of them were held at the Admiral's home, Jubilee Farm, Leonardtown, Maryland between August, 1971 and February, 1972.

Admiral Johnson made some minor corrections to the original transcript. It was then re-typed, indexed and bound. Essentially the text remains as it was spoken by Admiral Johnson on tape.

VICE ADMIRAL FELIX L. JOHNSON, UNITED STATES NAVY, RETIRED

Felix Leslie Johnson was born on July 15, 1897, in Aberdeen, North Carolina, son of James McNeill and Annie (Cockman) Johnson. He attended John Graham High School in Warrenton, North Carolina, and the University of North Carolina at Chapel Hill before entering the U. S. Naval Academy, Annapolis, Maryland, from the Seventh District of his native state in 1916. As a Midshipman he served during the summers of 1917 and 1918 in the battleships NEVADA and VIRGINIA (both operated with the Atlantic Fleet during World War I), and was Manager of the Academy Track Team. Graduated and commissioned Ensign on June 6, 1919 with the Class of 1920, he subsequently attained the rank of Rear Admiral to date from October 10, 1943. On September 1, 1952 he was transferred to the Retired List of the U. S. Navy and was advanced to the rank of Vice Admiral on the basis of combat awards.

Following graduation from the Naval Academy in 1919, he was assigned to the USS DELAWARE and was aboard that battleship during the Haitian Campaign in December 1919. Detached in December 1920, he continued duty afloat in the USS STEWART, USS STRIBLING, USS SUMNER, USS THATCHER, again in the SUMNER, and the USS PYRO, successively. He joined the USS PENGUIN when she was commissioned on October 13, 1923, and served on board while she operated on Yangtze Patrol until September 1925. He was then transferred to the USS RIZAL, and upon his return to the United States in June 1926, he reported as an Instructor in the Department of Navigation at the Naval Academy.

He was ordered to Asiatic Station in June 1928, and while enroute to China via the Suez Canal, served as Navigator of the schooner yacht ATLANTIC in the Spanish Ocean Race, New York to Santander. During September and October 1928 he had duty in the USS GENERAL ALAVA, and after brief service in the USS PENGUIN, reported on October 25, 1928, on board the USS PAUL JONES. He was detached from that destroyer in July 1929 for duty as Aide and Flag Lieutenant on the Staff of the Commander in Chief, U. S. Asiatic Fleet, USS PITTSBURGH, flagship. In July 1931 he was assigned to the Naval Mine Depot, Yorktown, Virginia, where he served until May 1933, and for three years thereafter he was at sea as Assistant Gunnery Officer of the USS TENNESSEE.

Following brief duty in the Office of the Chief of Naval Operations, Navy Department, Washington, D. C., he reported in August 1936 as a member of the Naval Mission to Brazil, Headquarters at Rio de Janeiro. He remained there until December 1938 and, after fitting out the USS LANG, assumed command of that destroyer upon her commissioning, March 30, 1939. In November 1940 he reported to the Navy Yard, New York, N. Y., where the SS CHALLENGE was being converted, and upon her commissioning on March 12, 1941 as the USS CASTOR, took command.

V. Adm. F. L. Johnson, USN, Ret.   Page 2

Detached from command of the CASTOR in July 1941, he was again assigned to the Naval Academy, this time as Secretary of the Academic Board and Aide to the Superintendent. He remained there during the early period of World War II, and in July 1943 assumed command of the USS PRESIDENT ADAMS. "For heroic achievement as Commanding Officer of the USS PRESIDENT ADAMS during the initial amphibious landing on enemy Japanese-held Cape Torokina, Bougainville Island, Solomon Islands, on November 1, 1943, and while landing reinforcements on November 8, 1943,..." he was awarded the Bronze Star Medal with Combat "V," the citation stating:

"Responsible for landing troops at the most fiercely defended point on the assigned beach, (he) directed his command with professional skill and aggressiveness. Although the landing craft from the PRESIDENT ADAMS bore the brunt of enemy fire and suffered heavy casualties in men and the loss of a number of boats during the opening phases of the assault, his highly disciplined and well trained crews, control personnel and beach parties carried out the mission of getting troops ashore with cool courage and determination..."

He also received the Ribbon for the Navy Unit Commendation awarded the USS PRESIDENT ADAMS for "exceptionally meritorious service in action against enemy Japanese aircraft, shore batteries, submarines and mines in the South Pacific Campaign...Under numerous attacks, the USS PRESIDENT ADAMS...contributed to the defense of other units by the performance of her battery against the enemy...(and) contributed greatly to the decisive victory achieved..."

In November 1943 he became Assistant Chief of Staff to the Commander South Pacific, with additional duty as Liaison Officer between the Commander South Pacific, Commander in Chief, Southwest Pacific and Commander SEVENTH Fleet. "For exceptionally meritorious conduct (in that assignment) from November 27, 1943, to May 15, 1944..." he was awarded the Legion of Merit. The citation continues:

"Rear Admiral Johnson rendered invaluable assistance in the formulation and execution of policies in connection with the base planning for the Manus Island operations and, by his keen initiative and thorough understanding of naval warfare, contributed materially to the strategical employment of South Pacific forces and the transfer of troops and equipment from the South Pacific Area to the the Southwest Pacific Area. His unfailing tact, tireless efforts and conscientious devotion to the varied and complex details of this vital assignment were essential factors in the successful prosecution of the war..."

He returned to the United States in June 1944, and after the fitting out of USS SPRINGFIELD, commanded that cruiser from her commissioning on September 9, 1944, until May 15, 1945. In January 1945 the SPRINGFIELD provided escort protection for the late President Franklin D. Roosevelt's party during the trip to Yalta to meet with Churchill and Stalin. She then joined Cruiser Division SEVENTEEN in the Pacific and operated as a part of Fast Carrier Task Force FIFTY-EIGHT of the FIFTH Fleet, participating in powerful air strikes against Kyushu, Honshu (March 18-19, 1945), and from March 23, fought in the bitter campaign for the island of Okinawa. During the Okinawa operations she took part in two bombardments of Minami-Daito Shima (March 27-28 and May 10-11); and engaged in another series of strikes against enemy air bases in Kyushu on May 13-14.

On June 29, 1945, Admiral Johnson was assigned to the Bureau of Naval Personnel, Navy Department, Washington, D. C., and on January 9, 1946, became Assistant Chief of that Bureau. He continued to serve in that capacity until November 4, 1946, when he was designated Director of Public Relations, Navy Department. That tour of duty completed, he reported in March 1948 as Commander Destroyers, U. S. Atlantic Fleet. He was detached from that command in September 1949 upon his designation as Director of Naval Intelligence, Navy Department, in which assignment he served until relieved of all active duty pending his retirement on September 1, 1952.

In addition to the Legion of Merit, the Bronze Star Medal with Combat "V," and the Navy Unit Commendation Ribbon, Vice Admiral Johnson has the Navy Expeditionary Medal; World War I Victory Medal, Atlantic Fleet Clasp; Haitian Campaign Medal; Yangtze Service Medal; American Defense Service Medal, Fleet Clasp; American Campaign Medal; Asiatic-Pacific Campaign Medal with two operation stars; the World War II Victory Medal; and the National Defense Service Medal. He is a Commander of the Legion of Honor (France), A Commander of the Order of Naval Merit (Brazil), and an officer of the Order of Naval Merit (Chile).

On January 18, 1954, Secretary of the Navy Robert Anderson appointed Admiral Johnson to succeed the late Admiral W. H. P. Blandy as Chairman of the Naval Reserve Evaluation Board. This Board was created in the fall of 1953 to "critically examine the mission of the Naval Reserve, including Air, as it relates to the needs of the Navy and to the broad aspects of National Defense." Recommendations by the Board were made to the Secretary in August 1954.

In February 1956 he was appointed Chairman of a Board to evaluate and make recommendations concerning the promotion system for Naval Reserve Officers. Recommendations by the Board were submitted to the Secretary in September of 1956.

On August 1, 1961, he was recalled to active duty, assigned as Chairman of the Naval Reserve Evaluation Board, Navy Department, Washington, D. C. and remained there until June 8, 1962, when he was relieved of active duty.

Admiral Johnson is married to the former Fay Doyen of Annapolis, Maryland, and they have two daughters, Doyen and Felicia. The family residence is "Jubilee Farm," Leonardtown, Maryland.

Navy Office of Information
Internal Relations Division (OI-430)   6 March 1970

DECLARATION OF TRUST

The undersigned does hereby appoint and designate as his (her) Trustee herein, the Secretary-Treasurer and Publisher of the United States Naval Institute to perform and discharge the following duties, powers, and privileges in connection with the possession and use of a certain taped interview between the undersigned and the Oral History Department of the United States Naval Institute.

1. Classification of Transcript.

   (✓)a. If classified OPEN, the transcript(s) may be read or the recording(s) audited by the qualified personnel upon presentation of proper credentials, as determined by the Secretary-Treasurer of the U. S. Naval Institute.

   ( )b. If classified PERMISSION REQUIRED TO CITE OR QUOTE, the user will be required to obtain permission in writing from the interviewee prior to quoting or citing from either the transcript(s) or the recording(s).

   ( )c. If classified PERMISSION REQUIRED, permission must be obtained in writing from the interviewee before the transcribed interview(s) can be examined or the tape recording(s) audited.

   ( )d. If classified CLOSED, the transcribed interview(s) and the tape recording(s) will be sealed until a time specified by the interviewee. This may be until the death of the interviewee or for any specified number of years.

2. It is expressly understood that in giving this authorization, I am in no way precluded from placing such restrictions as I may desire upon use of the interview at any time during my lifetime, nor does this authorization in any way affect my rights to the copyright of my literary expressions that may be contained in the interview.

Witness my hand and seal this _____ day of _____ 19__.

_____

I hereby accept and consent to the foregoing Declaration of Trust and the powers therein conferred upon me as Trustee:

_____

Vice Admiral Felix L. Johnson

Jubilee Farm, St. Mary's County, Maryland

August 31, 1971

By John T. Mason, Jr.

Mr. Mason: I have indeed been looking forward to this, Admiral Johnson. I have met a number of your friends and all of them extol your virtues, and so I have really felt that this would be a great privilege to meet you and to hear your story of your illustrious naval career.

In the manner of all good biographies, I wonder if you'd be willing to start with some statement on your family background and your early education, something of that sort.

Admiral Johnson: In fact, I'll be very happy to.

I was born in a little village called Aberdeen in North Carolina. It's a little village in the Cape Fear Valley which was settled by Scots in the great exodus from Scotland in the 1700s.

My father was a farm boy. When he married mother she was sixteen and he was twenty-four. He was a turpentine cutter. He strips the trees, cuts the bark from the trees and draws off the turpentine. He had had one and one-half years of schooling at that time.

A little later he started a little country store, and he didn't feel that that was stimulating enough so he studied pharmacy by mail and became a pharmacist, and started a little drug store in Aberdeen, the first drug store. After a few years of that he felt that there were many limitations in that so he left mother and her sister to run the store - he had five children by this time - and went away to college. He went to Wake Forest College.

Mr. Mason: What an enterprising young man!

Admiral Johnson: Wasn't he an amazing man?

Mr. Mason: Where did he get the funds to go?

Admiral Johnson: From what mother made on the drug store. That had to support him and the family there.

Mr. Mason: I would surmise that perhaps his initial beginning as a turpentine cutter led him into the drug area.

Admiral Johnson: I think it probably did, yes.

In a year and a half at Wake Forest he got an A.B. and a law degree. Then he came home and gave up the drug store and started the law business and became a very distinguished lawyer. He was an excellent speaker, he was a surveyor, a poet, historian, and I think he was a most wonderful man.

He was a devoted Scot, and went back to Scotland whenever he could. I think it's from him that I inherited my love for

Scotland. We spent two months there this spring.

Mr. Mason: What a father! Tell me a little about your mother.

Admiral Johnson: My mother was the daughter of an old Confederate soldier. My grandfather was Mark Cockman; she was his daughter. He was a calvaryman under Jeb Stuart. She came from the next county, and while she did not have the education and opportunities that my father had or made she was a perfectly wonderful woman and a marvelous partner.

Mr. Mason: She would have to be in order to encourage him to do that.

Admiral Johnson: Yes, and marrying at sixteen years of age.

I went through the little school of Aberdeen. There wasn't such a thing as a grammar and high school in those days; there was just one school there. They only had ten grades. I graduated from tenth grade when I was fourteen, I believe.

Then, I went to the John Graham High School in Warrenton, North Carolina - a splendid boys school, a boarding school - run by John Graham, who was a great Latin scholar. I was there for a year and a half . . .

Mr. Mason: Where did you rank in the family of five?

Admiral Johnson: I was next to the youngest. There was a sister, then a brother, then another sister, then I, and then my younger brother.

Mr. Mason: Did the older ones also . . .

Admiral Johnson: The older ones all went to college. My oldest brother also became a very distinguished lawyer, and my father's law partner. He died this year at the age of eighty-three. My two older sisters both have died too, but both were college graduates. They went to what is now called Flora MacDonald College at Red Springs, North Carolina. It was just called Red Springs College in those days. It was settled by the Scots and founded by the Scots. My younger brother had some difficulty with his college but eventually got through a college called Bowie's Creek College in North Carolina. It was a junior college. He and I are the only ones that are now living.

I went to Warrenton to the Graham School for a year and a half. Then I had seen a girl at home who had a Naval Academy belt buckle. I was very much in love with another girl at that time and I thought what a killing I could make if I could give her a belt buckle. This girl with the belt buckle told me it had been given to her by a midshipman at the Naval Academy, so I determined to go to the Naval Academy.

Mr. Mason: On the basis of a belt buckle.

Admiral Johnson: I guess so.

Mr. Mason: And some other convictions as well, I'm sure.

Admiral Johnson: Having determined to go to the Naval Academy I decided that some special preparation was necessary so I got my father's permission to go to Annapolis and attend the Werntz's Preparatory School - Bobbie Werntz's War College as it was called.

Mr. Mason: Incidentally, how did your parents react to this idea?

Admiral Johnson: They thought it was fine. My old military grandfather encouraged them in it, he thought it would be fine to have a grandson in one of the services. As a matter of fact he was still living then.

Mr. Mason: But actually there had been no naval connection.

Admiral Johnson: None whatsoever, none at all.

So by the time I got my belt buckle I'd forgotten who the girl was and she'd forgotten me, but it started me anyway.

I took the examinations in April of that year, 1915, and passed them, but was unable to get an appointment. I only had an alternate appointment. So I had to kill a year and in order to do that I went to the University of North Carolina for about three-quarters of a year.

Mr. Mason: That was really killing at a good advantage.

Admiral Johnson: Very good advantage because I tried to take things that would help me most at the Naval Academy.

Mr. Mason: Having gone to Bobbie Werntz's School you had some concept...

Admiral Johnson: Yes, I did, of what was going to be required there.

At that time for some reason the product from North Carolina at the Naval Academy did not do well at all. Most of them were having a great deal of difficulty getting through.

Mr. Mason: Because of the educational background?

Admiral Johnson: Because of the lack of education facilities in North Carolina.

I got in in 1916. My congressman was Robert N. Page, a member of the Page family of my area, one of whom became the wartime ambassador to the Court of St. James - Walter Hines Page. This was his brother who appointed me to the Academy.

I entered in 1916 and one of the first blessings that came to me was the roommates that I got. I roomed with two from Massachusetts and one from Arkansas - perfectly wonderful, delightful, helpful, charming, able men. They helped me so much through those years there. We had a reunion down there last year, all four of us were there. One came from Arizona, one from Annapolis, one from California - we had a reunion there.

So I had an undistinguished career at the Naval Academy. I was not an athlete. I tried to be a track man; I was the manager of the track team.

The course was reduced to three years during the war - one of those speed-up courses. One of those summers I went to sea in the USS Nevada, most of the time was spent in the York River at Yorktown, Virginia or around in the Bay. We made one quick cruise out into the Atlantic. The next summer I was on the battleship Virginia. Then I graduated in 1919 . . .

Mr. Mason: Did those summer cruises do anything for you in terms of solidifying your determination to be a naval officer?

Admiral Johnson: They did indeed, yes. They were fascinating.

Mr. Mason: They were coal-burners, were they not?

Admiral Johnson: The second one was, the Virginia was a coal-burner. I didn't like coal-burners and never did.

Mr. Mason: It was kind of hard work, wasn't it?

Admiral Johnson: A relic of barbarism - a coal ship is. That's a dreadful thing. The Nevada was an oil-burner, so I could see how much easier it could be.

I graduated and . . .

Mr. Mason: Before you talk about that era, tell me your recollections of courses, and their value to you.

Admiral Johnson: That's so long ago now. I did quite well in everything but mechanical drawing. I was very bad in mechanical drawing - I got about a 2.8 or 2.9 or something like that. I did fairly well in the rest of the things. I think I stood 69 in a class of 450 - that was largely because I had been to the University of North Carolina.

Mr. Mason: That was a great advantage, wasn't it?

Admiral Johnson: Oh, terrific. I would recommend to anybody to do it.

Mr. Mason: In the light of that experience and what other men had - similar experiences - who went to college, if the powers that be in the Navy hadn't considered making the educational requirements greater for them . . .

Admiral Johnson: I think they are greater now. As will come out later I was the Director of Admissions at the Naval Academy for two years - that's much later - and had we had the same requirements when I came in that they had then I don't think I would have made it.

I loved the Naval Academy. It was pretty strict in those days. We had twenty-four hours off for Christmas, and had about three weeks off in the fall - that was the only time.

Mr. Mason: No freedom outside the Yard?

Admiral Johnson: You were allowed to go out in town - plebe year you were allowed to go out one Saturday afternoon a month. The next year we were allowed to go out every Saturday afternoon. And the first class year we were allowed to go out every afternoon after the three o'clock period was over - that gave us about an hour and a half outside.

I got to know some civilians in town near where you live now. My last year there I met my wife, whose father was a General in the Marine Corps. He had taken the First Marines to France during the war and had died shortly after he returned. She was living in Annapolis with relatives. That was the best thing that ever happened to me - when we got married.

Mr. Mason: And your class was a fairly distinguished class, was it not? I mean - a number of you succeeded in making your mark.

Admiral Johnson: We had quite a number who became flag officers.

I don't know any who will be remembered forever for what they did for the Navy. Two of them became four-star admirals. Wooldridge was a three-star admiral, and he became four-stars when he retired.

I'm not truly a Vice Admiral, I became a Vice Admiral when I retired. That's a combat citation.

Wooldridge was one of the most distinguished members of the class, possibly the highest position that he ever held was President of the National War College.

Hillenkoetter was another Vice Admiral, he never became four-stars.

The two that became four-stars were Curts and Hopwood. Curts was Commander-in-Chief Pacific Fleet, and I think Hopwood held the same job.

There were quite a number of Vice Admirals in there, and we had about fifty flag officers in the class. Of course, many didn't like the life and resigned as they went along.

Mr. Mason: Actually, does not the summer cruise act as something of a culling out . . .

Admiral Johnson: It certainly does. It teaches them what they're going to face, and what they're going to find out.

Mr. Mason: This is a practical application, isn't it?

Admiral Johnson: Very practical application.

We were speaking a little while ago about having been to college and to preparatory school -- if I were laying down the rules I would make it a requisite that they have attended some school away from home before being at the Naval Academy. The number who get desperately homesick is appalling, it really is. Some don't make it, many resign.

I note that the figures from the Naval Academy the other day - of the thirteen hundred that entered about the first of July about thirty-nine resigned the first week. It was too rigorous for them.

I had a dreadful thing in my class; a boy from Pennsylvania who had been in I think eleven days (I knew him, he roomed near me) and he got desperately homesick. He was put on report for missing a formation, or being late for a formation. That was a tiny little thing, that just meant the end of the world to him. So that noon when the whole regiment of plebes was lined up in front of Bancroft Hall he climbed on top of Bancroft Hall and jumped off with the whole regiment looking. He hit across the rail there and was crushed. It was a dreadful thing.

Mr. Mason: Admiral, did you have any choice in determining what your first tour of duty would be?

Admiral Johnson: We drew numbers, and the man who got the first number could take his choice of every vacancy in the Navy. I got a rather low number so I drew the Delaware, which was a fine ship but it was a coal-burner and that was not very desirable.

Fortunately, one of my roommates also went in the Delaware, and we roomed together on the Delaware.

Mr. Mason: The important thing was that you have a good skipper?

Admiral Johnson: We started out with a wonderful skipper named Reginald Belknap. Have you ever heard of him?

Mr. Mason: I knew him.

Admiral Johnson: You did, really? What a man!

I joined the ship in New York and so did he. And we got underway to head down the North River heading for Massachusetts. I was on watch on the bridge and I drew my first commissioned assignment in the Navy. He asked me if I had a handkerchief, and I did, and he stationed me in the wing of the bridge and I had to wave at the populace of New York from the bridge of this ship as we steamed down the River. I was somewhat humiliated at being charged with this duty, but I did it anyway.

Mr. Mason: Admiral Belknap was ever mindful of the need for public relations.

Admiral Johnson: Oh, he was indeed.

We went to Rockport, Massachusetts directly - I still love Rockport - and we anchored there. A day or so after we had anchored we got an order from the Bureau of Personnel to release anybody in the crew who had signed up for the period of the war and wanted to get out. So our crew in about three days dropped from somewhere around twelve hundred to about three hundred and fifty - that's all we had left.

Mr. Mason: Was twelve hundred the full complement?

Admiral Johnson: Twelve hundred was the full complement, yes.
So we couldn't get underway. We stayed there for about two months during which we were required to go up through New England. We made up two baseball teams and went around from village to village in New England playing exhibition baseball games and then making a speech, trying to recruit people to the ship, and we got enough people in that way.

Mr. Mason: That was direct recruitment.

Admiral Johnson: That was direct recruitment.

Mr. Mason: You must have had a good baseball team.

Admiral Johnson: We had a very good baseball team, we certainly did.

I enjoyed Admiral Belknap very much. Do you possibly remember he was the officer in charge of the North Sea Mine Barrage? That was the great event of his life, and he loved to talk about it. He had, I think, five daughters at that time - we all liked his daughters - and an awfully nice wife.

Mr. Mason: Tell me Sir, was that not rather demoralizing for the young officers on board to have the crew just dissipated?

Admiral Johnson: It was very demoralizing for us. Captain Belknap put us to work raising a new crew - everybody had something to do with this effort of raising a new crew - and that managed to tide us over, but it was not good for us at all. It wasn't good for us to stay so long in this place; it was a delightful place. They had a good golf course there and I started to play golf; I learned to play golf there. But it was not good for us.

This had happened to the whole Navy, it wasn't just my ship, but the whole Navy just went down and lost these people. I suppose in a period of a week we lost two-thirds of our crews.

Mr. Mason: I would think it would have made each and every one of you who planned on the Navy as a career to begin to reassess your prospects.

Admiral Johnson: It probably did. I think the Navy did not let any of my class resign that summer. As I remember it we had to do a year before we could resign.

Adding to that, I can remember one feeling that I had about it. There were so many officers there, so many far far senior to me, that I had the feeling that I wasn't doing anything which required very much responsibility. So I was glad when the time came that I could leave the ship and go to a destroyer where there are so few officers and where each officer bears a correspondingly much greater responsibility.

Mr. Mason: What, for instance, did you derive from the example of Admiral Belknap? What did you get from him as skipper of the ship?

Admiral Johnson: He's the coolest shiphandler I ever saw. He was a very able seaman, never got excited.

We had a wonderful executive officer named Captain Sam Loomis, now retired, and I learned a great deal from him. He was wonderful in his understanding of men's problems, his patience in discussing them, not a tyrant of any kind. I had a division officer, Ford Wilkinson, a delightful gentleman of whom I was very fond. He was of the class of 1918. Slim Wooldridge was a shipmate and roommate of mine aboard the Delaware.

But I was pleased really when the time came that I could leave the battleship and go to a small ship where I had a great deal more to do.

Mr. Mason: What kind of duties did they give you on the Delaware?

Admiral Johnson: I was first the junior officer in turret five, fifth division, which manned the aftermost turret of the ship. I did that for about nine months, and then I was transferred to the engineering department where I was the junior officer in B division. B division is the one which handles the boilers of the ship. I was also the bunker estimator when they coaled ship. I had to crawl in and out of all the bunkers in the ship about once an hour to estimate how much coal had come on board.

Mr. Mason: You must have been fairly slight of build.

Admiral Johnson: I was slight of build, and a mass of blackness by the time I finished, of course.

Mr. Mason: Since this was the time of the early, very early beginnings, of Naval Aviation, were you at all tempted to explore that field?

Admiral Johnson: I don't think I was. Several of my classmates, after one year in the ship, did go to aviation. I had my first flight during that year in Norfolk in what would later be a PBY, a big seaplane, and I thought it was pretty rough and crude and was not intrigued by it somehow, so I never really thought of volunteering for aviation.

Mr. Mason: You wouldn't have gotten much encouragement anyway from the senior officers.

Admiral Johnson: No, I don't think I would. No, none of them had had any aviation experience at all.

I never did particularly desire it. Of course, I've done a great great deal of flying in the back seat, but never as a pilot.

Mr. Mason: Tell me sir, how did the novice crew work into the situation?

Admiral Johnson: Just fine. They were all fine, enthusiastic, young New England lads.

The Navy Department, of course, was meanwhile sending to sea quite a lot of its petty officers who they had in shore jobs. We did get reenforcements that were qualified. But having these young lads who had just been recruited I think put more responsibility on us to supervise their work more carefully than we had been doing before.

Mr. Mason: How long did they sign up for?

Admiral Johnson: They had to sign up for either three or four years, I think it was for four years.

Mr. Mason: This also coincided with a kind of an economic

depression.

Admiral Johnson: It was, yes, an economic depression.

Mr. Mason: So not only your baseball team, but . . .

Admiral Johnson: The depression helped to recruit them for the ship.

Mr. Mason: Tell me about going to a destroyer.

Admiral Johnson: I requested duty in destroyers. I remember my Captain at that time was another man whom I liked very much, Captain Tompkins. Have you ever heard of him? He had a son named Rutledge Tompkins. John T. Tompkins was the father. Rutledge Tompkins, his son, was one year after me, he became a Captain in the Navy, too. I was very fond of this Captain. I wasn't there long with him. I told him of my desire to go into destroyers and he very kindly approved my request.

I went to Charleston where I was assigned to the destroyer Stewart in the Reserve Fleet.

Mr. Mason: Sir, before you talk about that - your biography says that you were aboard the battleship during the Haitian campaign in December 1919. Would you tell me about that?

Admiral Johnson: This was really a very interesting experience. Just before Christmas the Delaware was ordered to go to Haiti and to Santo Domingo to return quite a lot of Marines to the United States. I think they probably didn't have any transports in those days, so they were just using the Delaware as a transport.

We went to Santo Domingo first, Santo Domingo city. I remember we steamed in and as junior officer of the watch I saw a cruiser that looked like it was sitting up on the land. This was an astounding thing - I had not heard of or had forgotten that the cruiser Memphis had been washed ashore in a hurricane, I believe it was in 1914 or '15. She was still sitting perfectly upright in the middle of the rocks, about a half mile inland. I just thought she was anchored, but couldn't see how she got there. That was my first recollection of Sango Domingo.

Mr. Mason: We never bothered to try and get her off the rocks?

Admiral Johnson: No, she was too far and they couldn't move her.

We picked up a great many Marines, I should say seven or eight hundred there. Then we went around to the lower part of the island into Haiti and picked up a lot of Marines there, probably another thousand, and took them back to the United States.

Remember the United States at this time had occupied both Santo Domingo and Haiti, and we were doing a withdrawal then something like we're trying to do in Southeast Asia now.

Mr. Mason: Less fanfare then.

Admiral Johnson: Yes, no fanfare at all.

I remember very little about Haiti, except it's the first place I ever had a drink. I was raised in a teetotaling family, and I had finally decided it would be better to be a temperate than be a total abstainer. So I went out to call on a Marine family there and they offered me a cocktail, and with great trepidation I took it. And it wasn't so bad.

We came back to the United States and entered the river going up to Philadelphia and arrived two days before Christmas, and discharged all these Marines two days before Christmas.

Mr. Mason: Belknap was still skipper, was he?

Admiral Johnson: Belknap was still skipper, yes, at that time.

Mr. Mason: He was admirably suited I would think to deal with representatives of foreign governments. It was one of the characteristics of a naval officer in those days.

Admiral Johnson: It certainly was. A great many of us at that time held diplomatic positions. As an example, the Governor of Guam was quite a difficult job that was held by the Navy for so long. And the first Governor of the Virgin Islands was a naval officer.

Mr. Mason: That leads me to a question about the training at the Academy in your time. Was there any attention to this prospective role of the naval officer in preparation for this role?

Admiral Johnson: I think the performance of our predecessors who had done good jobs was related to it, but I don't believe we got any instructions other than the example - go forth and do likewise.

I never had a diplomatic job, and I was never an attache anywhere although I had all the naval attaches under me and visited them in many many countries - this is much later when I was an officer in Naval Intelligence. I very much enjoyed my relations with them.

I don't think that we had any particular training of that kind.

Mr. Mason: That was an interesting episode at least before you left the Delaware.

Admiral Johnson: Yes, it certainly was.

I left in January, I believe, and went down to Charleston. This was not a happy episode - the life in a destroyer - because these ships were in reserve with much reduced complements. We had, I suppose, about sixty men on each ship, three officers and sixty men.

Mr. Mason: How big was she, how many tons?

Admiral Johnson: It was a twelve hundred tonner, an old four-stacker.

We had about sixty men, but we just had to work desperately to keep them up. We had no radio operator at all. I actually trained myself in radio, because I was the radio officer of the ship, enough to take a message if it were sent very slowly. And I operated at sea as radio operator.

Mr. Mason: What was the ship's mission?

Admiral Johnson: There was a mission to hold it together until the Navy could be expanded enough to man them.

Mr. Mason: It was kind of a maintenance.

Admiral Johnson: That's right, that's what it was, maintenance.

Mr. Mason: Was she attached to any particular fleet?

Admiral Johnson: The Reserve Fleet in Charleston. Captain

Court, I believe, was my Commanding Officer. (Alva B. Court)

Mr. Mason: Class of 1905.

Admiral Johnson: I think he was. You know them all, don't you?

And from Charleston, in the spring -- I was only there about four months, I think. And I loved Charleston, a most delightful city and charming people. Have you ever been there - to Charleston? It's a wonderful, wonderful, old southern city.

Mr. Mason: And I expect with an assignment like that you had more opportunity perhaps to know the local people.

Admiral Johnson: I did. I ran around with local people almost altogether - played golf with them and went to "Riddicks", the one little night club in town.

Quite a number of my classmates married Charleston girls. You know Admiral Holloway, of course. Admiral Holloway married one of the Charleston girls - Jane Hagood, the daughter of General Hagood, a perfectly wonderful person.

Then we went up to Newport for the summer. At Newport we were a little more active. We went out a little more, and I think we had a few more men on board.

About this time - I had never been to the West Coast - I got an urge to see the West Coast. They called for volunteers from the Atlantic Fleet that would like to go to the West Coast so I signed up. I got married that spring, and signed up for the West Coast and joined a destroyer called Stribling that was leaving Newport for the passage around to the West Coast. I joined her just for the passage.

Mr. Mason: Why were they depleting the Atlantic Fleet?

Admiral Johnson: They didn't have any Pacific Fleet at that time. They had never had a Pacific Fleet, everything had been in the Atlantic. They were just starting, maybe we were beginning to look at Japan, too. So they sent a great many ships from the East Coast around to the West Coast.

Mr. Mason: It was also the time when we were beginning to contemplate the disarmament treaties, and so forth.

Admiral Johnson: It was, yes.

I was detached from the Stribling upon arrival at San Diego and joined the USS Sumner, a four-stacker, 333, with a very tough, very wonderful captain named Donald Bradford Beary. Eventually he became head of the Naval War College. During the war he commanded the Service Force Southwestern Pacific. He had somewhat of a temper, but he was a marvelous ship handler.

Mr. Mason: You say he was a very tough captain.

Admiral Johnson: Yes sir, he kept us right under his thumb.

Mr. Mason: He was exacting in what . . .

Admiral Johnson: Very exacting, yes sir. If I were a minute late getting up on the bridge I could imagine what would have happened to me then.

Mr. Mason: That was precisely what you wanted?

Admiral Johnson: That was wonderful. It was wonderful training. About the best training that I can remember is following in the steps of Admiral Beary, and also watching his ship handling. He didn't do it very easily, he was always keyed up a little, he used the techniques however. So I learned a lot from him.

Mr. Mason: Did most of the young officers respond to this strict discipline?

Admiral Johnson: I think they did. They all liked it very much. We took great pride in our ship. The Sumner always stood well, It shot well. If we didn't we had to come up and explain to the Captain why, so we were all working on it all the time. It was a great privilege to serve under Admiral Beary.

Mr. Mason: And there was a Pacific Fleet in being then?

Admiral Johnson: Yes, there was a Pacific Fleet.

Mr. Mason: And it was based on what, San Diego?

Admiral Johnson: No, the destroyers were in San Diego and the larger ships were in San Pedro.

I was there for two years, I think it was, then I got restless.

There's mention of a ship called the Thatcher. I was just assigned to the Thatcher on a temporary basis to put it out of commission, and then I went back to the Sumner again. I think I did three months in the Thatcher putting it out of commission, and then back to the Sumner.

Then I requested duty on the Asiatic Station. My wife's father had been out there twice during his life and she liked it out there. I'd never seen it and I wanted to see it, so I just requested anywhere on the Asiatic Station.

I was sent to Pearl to be the executive officer of a gunboat called the Penguin. It was actually a North Sea mine-layer, sort of a tug it looked like. The Pigeon and the Penguin, the two of these, were converted in Pearl Harbor to gunboats. They had some guns put on and accommations were improved quite a lot for the men and myself. So we commissioned them in Pearl Harbor.

Mr. Mason: Tell me - what was the status of our naval base in those days?

Admiral Johnson: It was being built up pretty rapidly. I can't remember who the commander of it was then. They certainly gave us all the help, all the attention, that we needed in commissioning these two ships.

My Captain was named Gates, and the Captain of the Pigeon, who was in command of the two vessels together, was Captain Elwyn Cutts. We departed from Pearl with these two little things.

I had a wonderful old Chief Boatswain's Mate on board with a Swedish accent named Smith. I don't know what his name really was; I always thought Smith was an assumed name because he spoke with a very broad Scandanavian accent. He had been in sail, and there was quite a question as to whether we could make it from Pearl all the way to Shanghai with the amount of oil we were carrying.

Mr. Mason: They were pretty short-legged, weren't they?

Admiral Johnson: Very short-legged.

Mr. Mason: What was the overall length of the Penguin?

Admiral Johnson: I think it was one hundred and eighty-five feet.

Smith suggested hoisting a mainsail. So we somewhere stirred up a mainsail and got it cut to the right dimensions. We hoisted that and it added about a knot to our speed for a good part of the way. We made it in with somewhere around eight or nine thousand gallons of oil.

Mr. Mason: That was an ingenuous solution.

Admiral Johnson: It was.

Mr. Mason: Did the *Pigeon* do likewise?

Admiral Johnson: The *Pigeon* did likewise, yes.
It was the first time I had been a navigator which later became a great joy to me - navigation. I was doing a lot of navigation mostly just out of the book, following a form, and not quite understanding what I was doing. But we got there all right.

Mr. Mason: Did you stop enroute anywhere?

Admiral Johnson: No, nowhere at all, just the one step from Pearl Harbor to Shanghai.

Mr. Mason: You were becoming a part of the Asiatic Station?

Admiral Johnson: The Yangtze Patrol.
We had to have quite a lot of conversion work done in the dockyards at Shanghai - additional living facilities on board.
After that was done we spent the next two years steaming up

and down the Yangtze looking after the American rights, trying to protect missionaries when they had rough times . . .

Mr. Mason: Tell me about some of these experiences - they must be very fascinating.

Admiral Johnson: The gunboats, such as I was in, the Pigeon and the Penguin, could only go as far as Ichang, which is at the foot of the gorges. There we began to strike the rapids so we couldn't cruise there. We had two little gunboats called the Palos and the Monocacy which did the run on the River protecting American interests from Ichang up to Chungking.

Mr. Mason: Protecting American interests from what?

Admiral Johnson: From bandits. Some bandits and Chinese were beginning to take some cracks at us even then, and our job was to protect them if anything did happen. We put an armed guard on each American merchant ship running from Ichang to Chungking - I suppose that's about two or three hundred miles up there. An armed guard usually would consist of eight enlisted men and one officer.

I've made that run many times, and been fired on by bandits. That was the first time I was ever fired on.

Mr. Mason: What kind of guns did they possess?

Admiral Johnson: Nothing but rifles. I don't know that they had any machine guns.

But we had armour plate around the bridges of these little gunboats, so when the shooting started we'd drop the armour plate and there were slits in there where we could put our rifles to reply.

Mr. Mason: And you were escorting a merchant ship?

Admiral Johnson: Yes, I was escorting this merchant ship, that's right. It was the merchant ships that had these shutters on them. The Dollar Line had several boats that ran up through there.

Mr. Mason: Did they run the full length of the River, or . . .

Admiral Johnson: They'd run only to Ichang. At Ichang they would shift the cargoes into the bigger ships. The Butterfield and Jardine-Matheson ships had sort of a corner on the traffic of the River.

This was in the summer that we were up there. In the winters the water was so low that we had to drop down the River; we couldn't stay at Ichang. We had to go down as far as Hankow, or we'd be stuck for the winter up there.

Mr. Mason: Does this mean that commercial traffic . . .

Admiral Johnson: They stopped running through the winters up there.

Mr. Mason: Did you have any close calls during that time?

Admiral Johnson: We grounded many times in the River. It was a natural thing for you to ground. The channel in the muddy Yangtze is constantly shifting from side to side, with very few buoys. So we often ran aground, but we always managed to back off.

Mr. Mason: The same penalty then didn't apply . . .

Admiral Johnson: No, I don't think we ever told anybody about it.

Then we stopped and pulled merchant ships off that had no power. We were always a welcome sight to them.

Mr. Mason: You said you also looked out for American missionaries - What did you do for them?

Admiral Johnson: The American missionaries were pretty brave and a good group of people out there. For some of them, their hearts really weren't in it, but most of them were.

I had a particularly profound admiration for the Catholic missionaries, because when a Catholic missionary came to China he gave up his country for life. He never expected to go back when he went to Shanghai with no thought of ever returning. The Protestant missionaries had sort of a rotation. After, I think it was three, four, or five years, they got a years leave to come home.

Mr. Mason: Of course they had family obligations.

Admiral Johnson: They had family obligations, yes.

I had lived with missionaries in a number of places. At Ichang with Mr. Cooper - he had a beautiful colonial house. There's an old story told about that - I'm sure it was apocryphal. When the first missionary had built this beautiful house there was down in the corner of the compound a little chapel (about as big as this room). He had come out from home and written back to say "we have built this beautiful temple to God, and with the few remaining bricks have built ourselves a humble dwelling." The humble dwelling was about ten times as big as the chapel there.

Sometimes there would be difficulties between the oil companies too and the Chinese. Standard Oil was about our best customer out there. I, a number of times, had to land with landing parties to stay at the Standard Oil compound to guard it until the difficulty had quieted down.

Mr. Mason: Did they have oil wells there?

Admiral Johnson: No, they brought the oil in in tankers and sold it to the Chinese.

Mr. Mason: It was a commercial enterprise.

Admiral Johnson: Commercial enterprises, pretty much kerosene was used by the Chinese for lamps. Oil for the lamps of China - Pearl Buck describes them.

Mr. Mason: What was the main endeavor of the American missionaries there? Was it conversion, teaching, what was it?

Admiral Johnson: I think it was conversion.

Mr. Mason: The British missionaries had a different purpose I understand. They went in for medical . . .

Admiral Johnson: We went in for hospitalization, too.

My cousin, who lives at Mulberry Fields, is the daughter of a famous doctor named William Lennox. Dr. William Lennox was the greatest expert in the world on epilepsy. He, I think, spent six years in a hospital in Peking working on the Chinese. He was, I think, interested mostly in persuing this deep interest of his in epilepsy. He found a great many cases of it there and tried to help them. And a great deal of the missionary effort was unselfish, but part of it was not. It varied just as it does with naval officers - it varied between missionaries.

Then I was in Nanking with a simply wonderful man, Dr. Walter Loudermilk, who was a great forester. His great urge was to rebuild the forests of China. They had all been just decimated. He wanted, and did, plant many many forests. And he also taught forestry in Nanking University, he was head of the forestry department there. We had the privilege of living with them. His wife had been a missionary who was interested in conversion. And it worked fine for the two of them - she followed her pursuit and he followed his. We loved living with them.

Mr. Mason: Did you and Mrs. Johnson become skilled with the language?

Admiral Johnson: No, I'm sorry to say I did not. I could talk to a rickshaw boy and tell him to take me home. That's the kind of land where even if you're only a young junior lieutenant - I was getting about one hundred and forty dollars a month - you had a servant. I think we only paid about six dollars a month for a servant. We learned to order a meal . . .

Mr. Mason: The patrol to which you belonged - was this under the command of the Asiatic Fleet or what?

Admiral Johnson: Yes, it was one of the functions of the command of the Asiatic Fleet. Commander of the Asiatic Fleet then had the flag in the Pittsburgh, and he came into Shanghai and spent about three or four weeks there in the spring enroute to China. They were always going up to China, up to Tsingtao and Chefu. We saw the Admiral and the staff at that time, and then they stopped on their way south in the fall. They spent about seven months in the north -- the winter months in Manila, Hong Kong. southern Philippine Islands.

Mr. Mason: Those of you who were attached most immediately to the patrol didn't have much . . .

Admiral Johnson: We never got out of the Yangtze River.

Mr. Mason: How did the U. S. Navy undertake this task of patrolling the River?

Admiral Johnson: I think it happened back at the time of the Boxer Rebellion when many American compounds had been raided, and this was an effort to supply them with protection. My recollection now is that that's when it started.

Mr. Mason: It was a colorful assignment. Did it add actually to your knowledge as a naval officer?

Admiral Johnson: It helped in that I formed many friendships with foreigners. I learned how to get along with foreigners.

The British had Yangtze patrol too, and we would look after their interests if they didn't have a gunboat there. And they would look out for our interests if we didn't have a gunboat there.

I had many many friends among the British. I saw a lot of the French . . .

Mr. Mason: Did they also have patrol boats?

Admiral Johnson: The French had patrol boats, too, yes, a few. I think there were only three. I remember the Boudart de Lagre, the famous picture of it - the water went down very fast in the rapids one night and left it sitting on top of a rock about fifty feet above the water. It just precariously balanced up there, and somebody got a picture of it. Of course, the water came up again a week later and they got it off. It was still running around when I was out there.

Mr. Mason: This indicates a tremendous change - fifty feet.

Admiral Johnson: Fifty feet. In the gorges these tremendous floods come down, and it probably rises a hundred feet in a night there. And, of course, you're always in danger of running aground.

It was a fascinating life, and I'm so glad that I did have a crack at it.

Johnson #1 - 37

Mr. Mason: Was there an official Chinese government in existence in that area? Was this the time of the war lords?

Admiral Johnson: This was the time of the war lords, yes. And we were always afraid that Chiang So Lin - who was the war lord of the north - was going to come down and knock everything off the river. But there was a precarious balance between the northern war lord and Wo Pei Fu, who, I believe, was the other one at the time. As long as they were suspicious of each other they didn't bother us too much, but we never knew when it would happen. I think it was a great comfort to the foreigners living there to have us ready.

Sometimes there would be grievous disturbances. I remember one night at Ichang I was away on an armed guard trip up the river. We three officers took it in rotation going up the river - just like taking a watch. It was a watch of a week that it took to make this run up and back. The American Consul got word that a group was going to come in and try to take over the Consulate. So Herman Barter, later a Captain in the Navy, took the armed guard - I think it was forty men - and marched from the Standard Oil dock up to the Consulate and spent the night, and we had a few shots fired, but the Chinese underground conveyed word to the Consul the next day that the danger was over. So Herman marched back to the dock but some Chinese pursued him all the way. He had to walk backwards - it was about a mile and a half - and they had to fall back on the dock with the imminent danger they felt all the way. Very few shots were fired. I think the Captain finally fired off a couple of the ship's guns - three-inch guns - just up in the air with a big boom to chase them off.

Mr. Mason: What was the objective of the bandits, was it plunder?

Admiral Johnson: Yes, that's what they were after.

Mr. Mason: Then they had no respect for foreign lives.

Admiral Johnson: Oh, no.
We never had anybody killed. I think we had one or two men wounded, but we never had anybody killed all the time that I was there.
It was a romantic, stimulating existence. I felt it was useful at the time.

Mr. Mason: How much time could you spend with your family? Where was Mrs. Johnson stationed?

Admiral Johnson: She was a Marine, and she was an awfully good traveler. She was based in Nanking. When I went to Ichang for the summer she came to Ichang and lived with missionaries up there for the summer. Then that winter I went back to Shanghai and she came down to Shanghai and lived there.

I think it was early spring a message came from the States. I was detached from the Penguin and ordered to Manila to join a minelayer called the Rizal. We had two minelayers - the Hart and the Rizal. The Rizal, of course, being named for the Filipino patriot.

I spent six months in Manila and got to know the Philippines to some degree. My family were down there with me and enjoyed it very much.

Mr. Mason: What was the purpose of the Rizal, not as a minelayer but was she doing typographic work?

Admiral Johnson: No. It was a minelayer all ready to carry mines, and ready to lay them if an emergency came at any time. We had plans for mining Manila harbor. I think even then we were beginning to look toward Japan.

Mr. Mason: She was a potential enemy then?

Admiral Johnson: We were even thinking about it then.

Mr. Mason: Were there any visible signs of the Japanese Navy?

Admiral Johnson: Yes, we saw them in Shanghai a great deal. They always had ships in Shanghai, and usually up the River, too.

They were running the River, too.

We didn't have any close personal relations with them like we did the other countries. I had no Japanese friends, I'm sorry to say.

Mr. Mason: What was their attitude as naval people towards us?

Admiral Johnson: They ignored us, and I think we did them.

Mr. Mason: The little you saw of their ships – were they efficient ship handlers?

Admiral Johnson: Yes, I think they handled them very well indeed. I think their ships were not quite as advanced as ours – the equipment they had.

We made boarding calls on them every time – every time a Japanese ship came in when an American ship was there we always went out and made a boarding call, as we did on all foreign ships.

Mr. Mason: Were they extra cautious about letting you view equipment?

Admiral Johnson: Well, they never invited me down below to see anything at all, so I think probably they were.

Mr. Mason: They were very much noted for that some few years later.

Admiral Johnson: I think possibly the greatest values that I got out of the time at Manila was my association with the Army. We saw a great deal of the Army down there - the ones in Corregidor and Camp John Hay. Have you ever heard of Camp John Hay in Baguio? That is one of the most beautiful places in the world.

Mr. Mason: That was a recreation center.

Admiral Johnson: Yes.

I made many Army friends there, and stayed until June at which time I was ordered back to the United States and to the Naval Academy.

Mr. Mason: Was this something you sought?

Admiral Johnson: I had put it on my fitness report - there is a place on your fitness report where you put your preference for your next duty. I did not submit a special request but I put it on my fitness report that this was where I wanted to be.

I was awfully fortunate when I got there to be assigned to duty in the Navigation Department. And I became somewhat of an experienced navigator - teaching it as well as practicing it. I loved that very much.

Mr. Mason: And your family had grown by this time.

Admiral Johnson: We had two children, two little girls.

Mr. Mason: So this was an ideal spot.

Admiral Johnson: This was an ideal spot, and my wife's family had a house there which we lived in part of the time.

Mr. Mason: Since you got involved with navigation - the teaching of navigation - was Captain Weems around?

Admiral Johnson: Yes sir, Captain Weems was a teacher at the same time that I was, and developed his system at that time.

John Gingrich was quite an unusual character, an outstanding individual in the class. He attained probably his greatest fame through being Mr. Forrestal's aide at the end of the war. He was a teacher of navigation also, and I think that he and Commander Weems together developed this system which is known as the Weems System of Navigation.

Mr. Mason: This must have been terribly stimulating for you - being in this area you associated with him.

Admiral Johnson: It was, being in the area I associated with him.

That's what led to this wonderful episode - navigating a ship in a race across the Atlantic. I never would have gotten that if I hadn't been in this Navigation Department, never would have been accepted as the navigator. But that was later.

I loved Annapolis, and it was at this time that I wrote a story on the Yangtze Patrol for the Naval Institute and took it over with fear and trepidation. Captain Baldridge read it and decided they would print it; he liked it. So then he asked me if I would like to be the assistant editor of the Naval Institute. He didn't have any other assistant editor at that time.

Mr. Mason: Had you ever done anything in the literary way before writing this?

Admiral Johnson: No, none at all. You can look at it, I suppose it's still there, published in 1926.

There was a Mr. Cox there then. He was the one who ran the office and did all the work. And Miss Reardon - she was the secretary. She had been the school teacher of my wife when she was a child - a wonderful lady. Then Captain Baldridge and I - that was the staff.

Mr. Mason: Where were you located?

Admiral Johnson: It was in Mahan Hall. We had two rooms in

Mahan Hall.

I was the one who had to make up the magazine every month, and try to get the stories the right length to fit which I never did seem to be able to do. I'd come out with a blank page and then had to put one of those sort of tail end things.

Mr. Mason: What kind of membership did you have?

Admiral Johnson: I just can't remember, but it was very small. I hadn't been a member up to that time.

I stayed there as assistant editor until I left and went to sea again.

Mr. Mason: Tell me a little about your teaching experience.

Admiral Johnson: I loved that. The great charm at the Naval Academy then of teaching there was the small number of Midshipmen that you had in your section. It was only fourteen or fifteen that you had in a section. When you have a class of that size you can get to know every one of them -- what his capabilities are, and a lot about his personality. It's so much easier to teach than when it's just a group of faces out there.

Mr. Mason: And much more effective.

Admiral Johnson: Oh yes, it certainly is.

Do you know what "saavy sections" are? Do they still use that expression down there?

Every one is arranged in a section according to his ability in that subject. The first month of the year they just draw them blind. At the end of that month there's a total rearrangement. The fourteen who stood the highest in that subject that month - they move up to the number one section. The next fourteen are in number two section, and next fourteen in number three section, and so forth down.

Mr. Mason: And this is flexible.

Admiral Johnson: Flexible - it moves every month. If you have the brilliant ones one month -- they rotate the officers, too - you got from the first section down maybe to the bottom section. You only have these people for one month. You'll get them again sometime during the course. I got so I knew all the Midshipmen in the class, and what their capabilities in navigation were. And you can stimulate them so much more by knowing them and talking to them.

I went on the cruise with them that summer to San Francisco in the battleship Nevada.

Mr. Mason: Then what's the advantage - the brightest ones probably stay together all the time?

Admiral Johnson: They very nearly do. If you've got just bright ones there you can pitch a lot more at them in that month. The course which is taught to the first section isn't at all the same thing which is taught to the last sections, because the last sections just can't assimilate it that fast. So you talk in a different language almost when you talk to the first section than when you talk to the last ones.

Mr. Mason: Doesn't this build up some kind of a psychological factor though?

Admiral Johnson: I think they are proud of being in the saavy section and they struggle to get up there.

Mr. Mason: What about the fellows who are in the last section - how do they feel?

Admiral Johnson: They're struggling like hell to stay in the Academy.

I don't really know whether they have the saavy sections now or not - I think they do.

Mr. Mason: Was there any correlation between saavy sections members and later flag officers?

Admiral Johnson: I think there is. It's not fixed though.

Baldridge stood next to last in his class, and you find some perfectly wonderful people down there. But the senior ones have a better chance, yes.

Mr. Mason: Class standing has always been a great advantage, hasn't it?

Admiral Johnson: Oh yes, it's a tremendous advantage.

One thing - the way you are ranked when you join the officers list of the Navy is in accordance with your standing at the Naval Academy. The man who's one at the Naval Academy is at the top of that four hundred and fifty that come in. That's a great help - to be up there, to be senior. Whereas the last man - he's junior to four hundred and fifty. So it does help. Also it helps a great deal in asking for special assignments.

My saavy roommate - I think he stood eighteenth in the class - helped me tremendously there. He became a naval constructor. Where I stood I never could have gotten in the construction corps if I had wanted to. They're the brains that come from the top and go to MIT, and the ones who get other postgraduate courses. It helps a great deal to have a high class standing because that's checked on by the board which chooses to the ones to go to postgraduate courses.

Mr. Mason: Admiral, later on in your career, when you were assembling a staff, did you take note of the man's standing in his

Naval Academy period?

Admiral Johnson: Yes. I took more notice of what his reputation with the Navy was at that time. I could always look up his record in Washington.

Mr. Mason: Because there is such a thing as what we call late bloomers.

Admiral Johnson: A lot of them, and Halsey was the perfect example of a late bloomer. Wooldridge stood about forty-five, or something like that. Curts, who went further than Wooldridge did, stood about one hundred. And Hopwood, I think stood about three hundred, who went further than Wooldridge.

Mr. Mason: Very often, at least to the outside observer, as I am, it seems to relate sometimes to whom you know and with whom you have served.

Admiral Johnson: It certainly helps to have served with someone... I have a great admiration for Admiral Carney, and he's almost my closest friend. He made a tremendous change in my life.

But if I knew someone that I was considering for my staff and I looked up and saw that he had done a good job with Admiral Carney, he was my man. I'd think I was privileged to get him there. That is not the same with all the officers. Admiral Carney, I think, had very high standards.

This is another of my friends - Admiral Denfeld - and this is Admiral McVay - I was his aide on my next cruise.

Mr. Mason: He's the father of the present Admiral McVay?

Admiral Johnson: Yes, that was his only son, only child.

He was a small man, a tough little man. I learned a lot working for him.

Mr. Mason: Admiral, would you tell me, while you were on the teaching staff at the Academy, what percentage roughly were naval officers and what percentage were civilian career people?

Admiral Johnson: Of course, it depended largely on the department. In Navigation we were all naval officers. In Ordnance they were all naval officers. In Engineering I would say that ninety percent were naval officers. In Languages probably ninety percent were civilian. In English probably seventy-five to ninety percent were civilians. The discipline department were all officers and the staff, I think were all officers. But I would say that there were more officers than civilians. That's probably been reversed now, hasn't it?

Mr. Mason: Yes, I believe so.

But the thought comes to mind that you, as naval officers, came there to teach professional subjects. You brought with you a practical knowledge from aboard ship. How did you keep abreast of new theories in your particular area? How did you master this?

Admiral Johnson: I think with reading the Naval Institute Proceedings.

We have a great many lecturers come down to the Naval Academy to lecture to the officers there. I think at this time it was possibly every week, or every other week, and you went to many many of these lectures to try to get abreast of what's going on, and reading professional magazines. They had some wonderful speakers.

Have you ever been to chapel services at the Academy? I think that's one of the greatest things at the Naval Academy, that's marvelous. The inspiration of those people - so many young men, many of whom are discouraged get a lift.

I was there on Pearl Harbor day listening to Peter Marshall preach while the bombs were falling. Did you ever hear of his sermon? Most prescient thing I've ever heard.

I asked him the next year when I saw him about that sermon, and he said it was stranger than I thought. On the way down he had Mrs. Marshall and Mrs. Marshall's father and mother with him. He had his sermon all ready. About half way from Washington a sudden tap came on his shoulder that said, "Peter, you can't use that sermon." So he turned to his wife and her mother and father and asked them if they'd please be quiet, that he had to think of a new sermon between there and Annapolis. And that sermon was born in that half hour. In the sermon he talked about how tenuous is this hold on life -- how short it is; at that moment the bombs were falling. It almost gives me the creeps.

Mr. Mason: I heard him preach many many times.

You don't think that the compulsory angle of attendance at the Academy is detrimental at all.

Admiral Johnson: Not a bit, I'm all for it. There are those who wouldn't go if they didn't have to go, but I think you should be exposed to some kind of religion at that period in your life. You're not going to have to stick to it the rest of your life. But if it wasn't mandatory to go, I think most of them would lie in bed on Sunday. So I'm all for it.

In addition to the religious side is the moving ceremony. I don't see how anyone could but be improved by standing up there watching that group of wonderful young men march into chapel with the band wailing away on <u>Onward Christian Soldiers</u>.

Once when I was an aide there I took a British captain who had been a friend in China to chapel with me, and with the superintendent's permission had him stand up on the steps to review the Midshipmen marching. Just as the last Midshipman was marching in I turned around and looked at him, Ian Crawford, and the tears were just streaming down. He said, "Felix, I'm sorry, but your pagentry is just too much for me." Now that's bound to help anybody, I think.

And they've had some awfully inspirational men there, particularly Will Thomas who was fourteen years at the Academy. He was the greatest of them all.

Mr. Mason: Recently when the compulsory angle was under fire, the superintendent, Admiral Moorer, and others stressed the fact that young men training for command should have an understanding of religion because they will be dealing with men. This seemed to be a very pertinent point to make.

Admiral Johnson: I made it a point on the ships that I commanded to always attend service on Sunday and to read one of the lessons, to show the men that it meant a lot to me. I thought they would get something out of it.

I remember the morning after Bougainville and we had to bury quite a number of our people. There was a wonderful little Baptist chaplain and the marvelous sermon that he preached.

I might forget this when we get there, so I'd like to recall it now, if I may. The night before we went into Bougainville - I was on the <u>President Adams</u>, and just getting in the war for the first time. We had two thousand Marines on board, landing them in the morning, making our run in on a live volcano, which was an added pagentry to the whole thing. The little Baptist chaplain was giving communion to the men - most of them were all so steamed up.

He came up on the bridge and said, "Captain, I would like to give you communion." "I can allow you three minutes," and I knelt on the bridge and he gave me communion. I think that's the most moving communion I ever had in my life. And I've been in Westminster and St. Paul's and the Washington Cathedral and a lot of others. That's when they get down to basics . . .

Mr. Mason: I can understand.

You came to the end of your tour of duty at the Academy. You were there for what - two years?

Admiral Johnson: For two years. And I had not requested duty in China again but I put it down as third choice on my fitness report, and apparently they were having trouble to get anybody to go to China at that time, so they ordered me to China again.

Mr. Mason: I thought it was a very desirable spot.

Admiral Johnson: I thought it was too, and I loved it out there. I don't know why - maybe it wasn't very good professionally at the time. But they ordered me out again.

So we were scheduled to go, and about a week before I was due to leave Annapolis I went to a picnic one night with Admiral

Norman Scott, who was killed at Guadalcanal, a wonderful friend of mine. He was in the Seamanship Department. We were at a picnic down at Bay Ridge, and Norman Scott said that he had been asked by a friend in New York if he would like to go as the navigator of his yacht in a race to Spain. Norman said he couldn't get away to do it. I kept thinking about it after I went home that night and it sounded very tantalizing to me. So I called on him the next morning and asked him if he'd mind if I told this friend of his that I'd like to go.

Mr. Mason: And you, I take it, had a passion for sailing.

Admiral Johnson: No, I was no sailor. I barely can get a half-rater or a little sloop in or out. It was the navigation angle I think that intrigued me.

So Norman said he'd be glad to, and he called his friend in Boston, named Dudley Wolfe, and said that he thought I would like to go.

Dudley Wolfe said to him, "Now I know you Norman, but I don't know this man Johnson you're talking about. And I can't take somebody unless I know him, because there might be a conflict of personalities here. So if he wants to come up to Boston to see me, I'll see him.

As soon as I got that call I borrowed fifty dollars from my uncle and took off for Boston. I saw Dudley Wolfe and spent the night with him. He was a wonderful man. He was going to be the skipper, the owner of the Mohawk.

Mr. Mason: And he was a wealthy man?

Admiral Johnson: Yes. And he said he'd be glad to have me go with him. He took me down to the racing committee to sign me up as his navigator. The chairman of the racing committee was another man from Boston, named Charles Francis Adams, who was at that time also the president of a trust company. It was in his office there Dudley Wolfe took me. And he said, "Dudley, don't you know that in the small class - there's two classes, fifty feet and under - the Mohawk was forty-eight feet - and over fifty feet - you can't have a professional navigator. It has to be an amateur yachtsman." So my face fell terribly because I was thrown out then and there.

Mr. Adams noted my depression, I think, so he said, "I'll tell you - I'm going as the skipper of the schooner Atlantic, which is owned by Girard Lambert, the President of the Lambert Pharmaceutical Company. He just might need a navigator. Do you want me to call him?" I said, "I certainly do."

So he called Girard Lambert while I sat at the desk and said he had a young naval officer there who would like to go in his race. Girard said the same thing as Dudley Wolfe - he'd have to see me.

So instead of going back to Annapolis I went to Princeton. I was getting low on money by this time. I had lunch with Girard and talked to him about two hours, and he said he'd be glad to take me, and he said that Mr. Adams was going to be his skipper.

But I hadn't mentioned this to the Navy Department yet, so I think it was pretty brash of me to say I would go. Because my orders were to go the next week - the other way to China via Seattle.

Mr. Mason: You must have had a friend in the Personnel Bureau.

Admiral Johnson: Well, I found one. The next day I went down there. J. O. Richardson was the Assistant Chief of Bureau of Personnel. I asked permission to see him, and told him my tale, and God bless him, he said, "I think that that might be good advertising for the Navy, and that it would be good for the Navy to participate in something like that. Sure you can go."

He canceled my orders then and there. It was thirty days before they'd sail, and he gave me an assignment in New York for thirty days where the Atlantic was tied up. I went up there and rode the Atlantic around the harbor for several days. Then Mr. Adams came down and Mr. Lambert came down. We sailed from New York on the 7th of July. We didn't win the race, but had a marvelous time. It was the Spanish Ocean Race of 1928.

Mr. Mason: How many contenders were in it?

Admiral Johnson: I guess there were six in the big race, and five in the small race. It was for a cup given by the King of Spain. There was a different cup - one for the big race and one for the small one.

Mr. Mason: Was this a yearly affair?

Admiral Johnson: No, it had never been done before.

Mr. Mason: What induced King Alfonso to sponsor it?

Admiral Johnson: He was a very dedicated yachtsman himself, and I think he was trying to stir up some interest in it.

Here is a picture -- the after guard is the owner and his friends who live in the stern of the ship - there were five of us. And twenty-two in the crew who lived forward - the paid crew.

This was about a one hundred and eight foot three-masted schooner with tremendous masts. They were taken out of three famous facing yachts - J boats - to put in the Atlantic for this trip. They were one hundred and eighty feet high, too. They were taken out of the Resolute, Vanity, and Seacall.

It took us, I think it was, seventeen days and sixteen hours to cross. We had a lead of I think eighty miles with two hundred to go and carried our racing sail too long, and a storm came along and blew it all away and fouled the fore foot.

It took us twenty-four hours to clear it, and another yacht, the *Ileana*, passed us, and we came in four hours after her.

Mr. Mason: Your association with Charles Francis Adams didn't do you any harm, did it?

Admiral Johnson: Oh, it was a wonderful thing.

Mr. Mason: He very soon was SecNav.

Admiral Johnson: Within the year he was SecNav. I couldn't believe it. I picked up a paper in Manila one day and saw that Charles Francis Adams was Secretary of the Navy. He was always so very kind to me.

This is young Charlie (showing a picture) who is at present chairman of the board of Raytheon Company.

At certain years in the Navy during the war happy coincidences seemed to occur because of this. I was made the chairman of a board after I retired to look into the health of the Naval Reserve. The vice chairman was Captain Charles Francis Adams, Jr. which was wonderful.

Of course, I made many many friends on that trip who came in the Navy after the war started, which wasn't too long after that. Practically all the New York Yacht Club came into the Navy during the war. I have so much enjoyed my membership in the New York Yacht Club.

Mr. Mason: You went into Santander, didn't you, and were you entertained there?

Admiral Johnson: Yes, as we steamed in the Commander-in-Chief in Europe had sent a cruiser, the Marblehead, I think it was, down to receive us. I'm not sure of the name - it was a light cruiser.

We had a rather crafty old paid captain on board the ship, Captain Aason. Mr. Lambert said to him, "Captain, be sure and dip your colors to the cruiser when we pass." And he said, "Mr. Lambert, I don't like to dip my colors to these man o' war. They don't pay any attention to you as you go by." Mr. Lambert said, "Never mind, you dip your colors," he gave him the orders.

And when we were about two hundred yards away sailing up the harbor there was a blast of a bugle on board. The crew came pouring out and the guard and the band, and they manned the rail, which they only do for royalty and the President usually. The band played The Star Spangled Banner as we went by. We all stood up and cried, including Mr. Lambert and Mr. Adams, and even old Aason had tears running down. It was a very moving moment for me.

Just about that time a little thirty-foot motor yacht came alongside, a tall dark man stepped out on the deck, stuck out his hand and said, "I'm Alfonso." Everybody was so smitten down. Mr. Adams got his breath first and said, "Yes, Your Majesty, we welcome you, we recognized you." And he said, "I

Johnson #1 - 60

want you all to come to the house and have dinner with me tonight." So we did. It was all very stimulating for a young lieutenant to have something like that happen to him.

Mr. Mason: Then how did you return to the States?

Admiral Johnson: I kept on going, I went through Suez. I got permission from the Navy Department to go by Suez in a maritime ship. It took about three weeks for that. That was a delightful experience, too.

Mr. Mason: And Mrs. Johnson was deprived of all this?

Admiral Johnson: She went by ship to France. She had a friend in France who wanted her to visit her. And she came down to Spain and spent the week with me that I was there, and all the festivities. Then she went back to France, and I went on out. Then a month later she came out in a German ship via Suez. So she also has been around the world. We had our reunion in Shanghai.

Mr. Mason: You gave me a statement off tape that I think would be worth putting on - at this point you were taking advantage of unusual opportunities. Would you repeat it, sir?

Admiral Johnson: Yes. I think I said that the reason I like

to tell this story of the Atlantic Ocean race is that I hope my experience would encourage others to take advantage of opportunities out of the usual norm of our lives. If you have such an opportunity as that -- going to London as attache for instance would be one that would help. Going to any kind of a diplomatic assignment would be one.

I hope that this would encourage our young officers to see that so much good can come out of this. You're able to make friends for the Navy, and certainly you're able to make friends for yourself.

Mr. Mason: And simultaneously, it is an obvious thing -- it's a broadening experience.

Admiral Johnson: It's a broadening experience, indeed it is, yes. You talk a little different language when it's over than you did when you started.

Vice Admiral Felix L. Johnson   Interview #2
U. S. Naval Institute
Annapolis, Maryland
September 16, 1971

Mr. Mason: It's certainly wonderful to see you this morning, Admiral. . .

Admiral Johnson: I'm very happy to be back again.

Mr. Mason: . . . and have you resume your most interesting story. Last time you concluded with the account of the Spanish race which was sponsored by the King. This was back in 1928. Do you want to continue, sir?

Admiral Johnson: After the race we had a weeks festivities around Santander and Bilbao. And I was fortunate enough to find that Captain George W. Steel, our Naval Attache to Paris, had come down for this week, so through him I was able to secure my passage to China in the D'Artagnan of the Messagerie Maritimes Line.

After another weeks leave with my family in France, where they were staying at the time, I went down to Marseille and embarked in the Messagerie Maritimes ship and had a most delightful voyage all the way to Shanghai.

Upon reaching Shanghai and debarking, I reported to the Commander-in-Chief where I received orders and was assigned to the General Alva, which was the Admiral's yacht, in Shanghai. But I was only there about ten days after which I was ordered to the Penguin the same old gunboat which I had taken to China some years before, which had been on the river patrol all this time.

And now the Penguin was being ordered to Manila to serve as a minesweeper in Manila. So I sailed in her to Manila just for that voyage.

Mr. Mason: What were your duties . . .

Admiral Johnson: I was the executive officer and the navigator of the Penguin for the trip down - just temporary duty on board. Whereupon, after arrival, I was transferred to the USS Paul Jones as executive officer.

Mr. Mason: And this was to be a permanent duty?

Admiral Johnson: A permanent assignment, yes.

I had a very interesting, unusual captain, known as Ham Bryan, Lieutenant Commander Hamilton B. Bryan - a very dashing, personable man. And I owe a great deal to him because it was he who first gave me opportunities of handling the ship - going alongside docks and ships. Most people have their fingers on their number so firmly that they don't give the juniors very much of an opportunity. But Ham would let me go over and fuel without him coming aboard. That did so much for me when the time came for me to command my own ship later.

Mr. Mason: I suppose, Admiral, the fact that the captain of a ship is responsible for his ship regardless of who's operating it is a deterrent, isn't it, for the training of younger men?

Admiral Johnson: I think it is, because it takes a great deal of courage for a captain . . .

If I may shift just a moment -- This happened some time later when I was in command of a destroyer myself, coming in to Galveston at midnight. My division commander was later Admiral Denfeld. He was captain, later Chief of Operations, Admiral Denfeld. Having learned from Captain Bryan how much it meant to officers to have the opportunity, I had a practice in my ship of making one landing myself, the executive officer making the next one, unless it was a very, very difficult situation. This night we were coming in it was the executive officer's turn to make the landing. It required coming in the narrow channel at Galveston and doing a one hundred and eighty degree turn and coming back alongside. It was about midnight; I didn't know anyone was watching us at all. My executive officer was Lieutenant Red Williams - F. P. Williams - and he did a beautiful job and brought it alongside the dock with much more dash than I would have done, I'm sure. Whereupon I received a message from the division commander, "Congratulations on your beautiful ship handling."

I didn't think I could quite accept that, so I said, "Thank you, but the ship handling was done by the executive officer." Then he said, "Congratulations to you for letting him do it." That concludes the story.

Mr. Mason: And a very appropriate one for this type of command.

Admiral Johnson: I served in the Paul Jones for about eight or nine months, when I received orders as flag Lieutenant to the new Admiral, the new Commander-in-Chief who was coming out - Admiral Charles Butler McVay.

Mr. Mason: Tell me before you leave the Paul Jones - what kind of duty did she have during those months? Where did she go?

Admiral Johnson: We made one trip over to Japan, and several trips up to Tsingtao and Chefoo. We spent one summer, as I recollect it, in Tsingtao, which is the most beautiful port in China. We were in Hong Kong once. It was the normal duty of a destroyer. She was the flag ship of the destroyer squadron, flying the flag of Captain Gaylord Church, who was the Commander, DesRon 12. She possibly had more visits to foreign ports than the average destroyer.

I was then transferred to the Pittsburgh, which was the flag ship of the Asiatic Station at that time.

It might be of interest how this appointment came about as a flag Lieutenant. You will recollect that my skipper in the race to Spain had been Charles Francis Adams, who about a year after the race was made the Secretary of the Navy. I learned later that Admiral McVay had gone in to see the Secretary of the Navy to take his leave before going out to China, and he said, "Mr. Secretary, is there any thing I can do for you out there?" The Secretary thought a minute and said, "I've got a young friend out there, Lieutenant Felix Johnson. You might keep an eye on him." And Admiral McVay said, "Sir, I'm looking for a flag Lieutenant, and I can keep an eye on him better by having him close to me, so I'll make him my flag Lieutenant." So this arose from the race.

Mr. Mason: This refers to what you said last time about the man fortunate to make the contacts.

Admiral Johnson: Isn't it though, very fortunate.

Admiral McVay's predecessor, the Commander-in-Chief in China, was a very distinguished man, Admiral Mark Bristol, who had won so much fame in Turkey. He did a very kind thing for me - seeing my orders to the staff of Admiral McVay, who was not to arrive for six weeks, he ordered me to his staff so that I would have six weeks of experience when Admiral McVay got there, and it was a tremendous privilege to serve closely with him.

Mr. Mason: It would not only be a help to you, but it would be a help to Admiral McVay.

Admiral Johnson: It would, indeed. I knew so much more about the station after that six weeks on board than I did before.

Mr. Mason: What was your impression of Admiral Bristol?

Admiral Johnson: I thought he was a wonderful man, with a very much broader gauge than the average officer, I would say. He had had this diplomatic assignment in Turkey, I believe it was called the High Commissioner to Turkey. And so his interests embraced things beyond the purview of the average officer of those times. He had a delightful Chief of Staff, Kenneth Castleman.

Admiral Bristol was relieved by Admiral McVay, and I, of course, was present at the turnover ceremonies, and served with Admiral McVay as his flag Lieutenant for about a year and a half. This gave me the opportunity of meeting many foreigners in Shanghai and Tsingtao, accompanying Admiral McVay to Peking and meeting many distinguished people there, the same in Hong Kong.

Admiral McVay was a different type than Admiral Bristol. He was a little fiery, extremely able too, but demanding a very high performance from all his assistants. So that for me was also a great privilege, and one which I thoroughly enjoyed.

He had fortunately been a close friend of my father-in-law,

so he and his wife were very, very fond of my wife, who was Fay Doyen, the daughter of Brigadier General Charles A. Doyen, Marine Corps. So it was almost like serving with someone in the family.

Mr. Mason: This just happened to work out because . . .

Admiral Johnson: It just happened to work out.

Admiral McVay's son, Charlie McVay, was a classmate and close friend of mine. The Chief of Staff was Kenneth Castleman, a very gracious, charming man. It was a privilege to be with him for that time. And then Admiral McVay's Chief of Staff was Captain Roscoe F. Dillen, and that, too, was a wonderful experience.

Mr. Mason: Can you cite any specific events that would be of interest during that tour of duty?

Admiral, while you were on the Admiral's staff, were you beginning to be conscious of the Japanese naval operations or anything of that sort? This was in the late twenties, and there were signs already, were there not?

Admiral Johnson: Yes, there were signs. We saw that the Japanese Navy was on the increase, we saw it's ships more frequently in China. Of course, we always called on the Japanese ships when they came in - that was one of my jobs, too.

Mr. Mason: What was their attitude toward American naval officers?

Admiral Johnson: Apparently very friendly at that time. To the best of my knowledge we had no disagreements at all.

Mr. Mason: Were they secretive in their equipment, their ordnance, and that kind of thing?

Admiral Johnson: They never let us see any of it at all. We got to the quarterdeck and possibly down to the wardroom for a cup of tea, but that's as far as we ever got.

Mr. Mason: Were we equally so with them, when they came on board?

Admiral Johnson: In the Pittsburgh we didn't have a single thing to conceal because the Pittsburgh was an old coal-burning four-stack cruiser, so I think we let them see anything they wanted to. But I think we did not let them see our submarines or destroyers - they were more modern.

Mr. Mason: Were the Japanese engaged in those days in night operations or anything of that sort?

Admiral Johnson: I never saw any of those, no.

Johnson #2 - 70

Mr. Mason: In addition to the normal duties of the units of the Asiatic Fleet - the showing of the flag, protecting our nationals, and so forth - were we also concerned about hydrographic matters and gathering information of that sort?

Admiral Johnson: I remember that we made a survey of Manila harbor during this time - that's the only one that I know of. However, I believe one time when we went down to Zamboango with a destroyer we were asked to make a survey of that if we could.

I might say it was during this time when I was with Admiral McVay that at his direction I arranged for him to call on General MacArthur, who was the Commanding General of the Philippines at that time. That was the first time that I met General MacArthur, with whom I was to have close association in later life.

Mr. Mason: And he was then in command of the U. S. troops . . .

Admiral Johnson: Yes, in command of the U. S. troops in the Philippines. He was a very outstanding personality, of course. I think he scared me a little bit at first, but I got along with him.

We had a wonderful Governor General of the Philippines at this time, too, whom I met several times. We were privileged to know Dwight Davis, who had two charming daughters with whom Ensigns used to go around if they were lucky enough to beat out the Army. One of them later married the British Ambassador in Washington whose name I can't remember.

Mr. Mason: It must have been a delightful kind of colonial life out there.

Admiral Johnson: Oh, wonderful, yes. This was something back in the last century.

Mr. Mason: Give me a picture of it, will you?

Admiral Johnson: I think that we had something to do every night; there were so many things going on. Duties were not onerous. We played golf a couple times a week. We met a great many foreigners. I was particularly fond of the Italians there. The Italians were the friendliest of all the foreigners, I would say. There were many Frenchmen too, particularly in Shanghai. The Cercle Sportif Francais, which is the French Club in Shanghai, was quite the most delightful club that I had ever seen, and still is just about the same. There were tea dances there, two or three times a week, which the young officers went to. My wife was, and is, an awfully good dancer so that was a big pleasure for her. We associated with so many of the young foreigners - it was a rare privilege which I'm not sure our young people of today experience. There was really no war or very much talking of war at that time, so we didn't seem to be under the strains which people have to bear now.

Mr. Mason: That must have been a tour of duty that you were reluctant to leave.

Admiral Johnson: It was, except that I was ordered to a different kind of duty, but an equally pleasant and happy one.

The Rizal in which I had served earlier was a minelayer, and I had learned something about mines and had considerable experience in laying them, so when the time came for me to be ordered home from Admiral McVay's staff I was ordered to the U. S. Naval Mine Depot at Yorktown, Virginia.

Mr. Mason: Was this something you requested?

Admiral Johnson: I think I had requested it, yes. On our fitness reports we put choices, and I had put that on my fitness report.

Mr. Mason: The reason I ask is I was wondering if in the wisdom of the Bureau of Personnel they try to fit people to slots where they've had some experience.

Admiral Johnson: I pointed out that I'd had experience with mines, and they did order me there as the Mining Officer.

The Mine Depot at Yorktown is a perfectly wonderful place; it's out in the country. It was the first time since I'd left the Naval Academy that I'd had the privilege of living in the country. There were only, I think, nine officers there. It's

Johnson #2 - 73

on the York River. Practically all the mines which the Navy owned at that time were stored there. We were constantly overhauling them and fitting them out and moving many of them to a place called Hawthorne, Nevada.

That's where I acquired a love of duck shooting, and fishing. Of course, these were prohibition times, but occasionally we would find some friend who would bring us a little illegal whiskey and we'd have a party with that, but not very often, not much of a party.

My boss there was the man who would become my very best friend in the Navy, a very distinguished man, the ordnance officer at that time, Lieutenant Commander C. Turner Joy, with a delightful wife. He liked the same things that I did, and taught me a lot about playing golf. I loved to work for him.

I was also very fond of the executive officer, who was Commander H. W. Underwood. The first commanding officer was Captain B.H. Green, a firey little man, whom I was also very fond of, then Captain Russell Crenshaw. I was tremendously fortunate to have these people as my bosses.

Mr. Mason: Tell me -- what use did we put our mines to at that time?

Admiral Johnson: Only for practice, and to stock them at places around the world where they might be needed. They were Mark VIs, these were the mines that had been used by the Navy in the North

Sea Mine Barrage - ones which had not been planted or had been recovered and brought back to America and restocked at Yorktown. The firing devices were subject to corrosion; it was necessary for us to work over them. We also filled mines and bombs at Yorktown, because I think at that time it was the only place the Navy had for loading bombs with TNT. We had some one hundred and five magazines scattered throughout the several thousand acres of the reservation, and we were constantly checking them. Every Sunday morning I had to make a round of the Depot to check on the mines, and the temperatures of the magazines.

At that time the Williamsburg operation had very recently been started. We met many interesting people connected with Williamsburg and saw it get underway. I think that was just a tremendously imaginative thing for Mr. Rockefeller to do.

I don't know whether you've heard the story of Mr. Rockefeller starting that -- He was in the York River in his yacht one Sunday when he decided to drive over to look at old colonial Williamsburg. And while he was there he went to the Episcopal Church, Bruton Parish Church, the rector of which was Dr. Goodwin. After the service Dr. Goodwin, learning that this visitor was John D. Rockefeller, asked him if he wouldn't let him take him for a tour around the town and show him some of the things. Dr. Goodwin was a great history buff, so by the time he finished he had communicated some of his enthusiasm to Mr. Rockefeller. Before Mr. Rockefeller left he said, "Doctor, I will give (I think it was) four hundred thousand dollars to saving some of these places which are falling in disrepair here if it's never known that I had anything to do with it. It's to be a secret; it's to be done by you."

So Dr. Goodwin agreed, and shortly thereafter Dr. Goodwin began to shell out thousands of dollars to restore things around town, and he soon ran out of the four hundred thousand, and I think Rockefeller put up three million at that time. After about eight or nine months of this it became ridiculous and Dr. Goodwin went to Rockefeller and said, "Look, this is just a completely ridiculous thing. You must let me say where this money is coming from." And Mr. Rockefeller then agreed to it being known that he was financing it, and he had offered a bigger scale.

Mr. Mason: Was there an experimental station there also, experimenting with new types of mines, or studying new types?

Admiral Johnson: That was not being done down at the Mine Depot. I think it was underway, but at the Naval Ordnance Laboratory in Washington that the experiments were being made.

One of my tasks, a rather frightening one to me at first, was destroying thousands and thousands of mine detonating devices which had become unstable. We were afraid to keep them. We were to take several hundreds of them at a time in the middle of an old mine storage field, which was empty at that time, and run a wire through them, get over behind a barricade, put our hands over our ears, drop the plunger, and off it would go. There was not very much explosive in each one of them, together they made quite a blast.

Mr. Mason: Did Admiral Belknap continue to evince an interest in mines? Was there any contact with him while you were there?

Admiral Johnson: No, I saw one of his daughters at this time, but not Admiral Belknap.

I think I mentioned that he was my Captain in the <u>Delaware</u>; I think possibly my first interest in mines came from hearing him talk about the mine operations in the North Sea. I heard that many times because that was almost his invariable subject when he was asked to make a speech somewhere, and he did it well.

Mr. Mason: Did the British have comparable mines at that time? Did we have any contact with them?

Admiral Johnson: We did not at Yorktown, no. But I think that at the time of the North Sea Mine Barrage that they also had a mine which was comparable to ours which was being planted.

Mr. Mason: I suppose in this interim period between two great world wars there wasn't a great deal of incentive to move forward with some of this ordnance.

Admiral Johnson: Not at that time. Of course, I was a minor figure there, but it seems to me that I did not feel that any great danger was hanging over the world or that we had to move fast to avert a catastrophe.

Mr. Mason: As a matter of fact, you were there during the time of the Great Depression, were you not?

Admiral Johnson: I was there during the Great Depression; I remember that very well. I've thought of it several times when the President made his present freezing of prices. We were cut fifteen percent; our naval salaries were cut fifteen percent, and that seemed quite hard at the time. I don't know whether it's fair or not, but we passed that on. We had a maid in those days, and we've had very seldom since then. She got ten dollars a week, and I remember in our desperate financial straits we told her we had to cut her to nine dollars a week. So we did, and she accepted it with grace.

Mr. Mason: Did it have any effect on the operations of the Mine Depot?

Admiral Johnson: I don't think so, no. What we were doing was not a very expensive operation.

It was quite hard on us. There were very few things we could purchase because my salary was quite small anyway. I remember going to the Bank of Yorktown with great trepidation asking if I could borrow fifty dollars, which they were kind enough to lend me, and I think I paid it back all in good time.

I left the Mine Depot in 1931. I was conscious of not having served in a large ship since I left the Delaware eight or nine years before, so I requested battleship duty and was assigned to the USS Tennessee, the sister ship of which was the California. I served four years in the Tennessee.

Mr. Mason: She was part of what fleet?

Admiral Johnson: The Pacific Fleet, based usually at Long Beach, California. We made visits to San Francisco, we were at Pearl occasionally, we went to Bremerton. And one summer the entire Fleet went through the Canal and came to New York for the summer, and then went back through the Canal.

The Commander of the Fleet at that time was another remarkable personality, Admiral Joseph Mason Reeves.

I don't know whether you've ever heard of his famous drill . . .

Normally in the Navy the fleet is in port for the weekend, most of them are, and the captain inspects below decks Friday afternoon and inspects the upper decks and personnel on Saturday morning.

This day we had come in on Thursday evening, I think, all anchored and taking it easy in Long Beach harbor. Friday afternoon came around - most captains were inspecting below decks;

a few of them had decided they would not do it that week-end and had gone ashore to play golf or for something else, when a signal came out from the flag ship to the fleet, "U. S. Fleet get underway and proceed to sea immediately."

That really threw us into consternation. We thought war had been declared.

We were all underway I would say within half an hour or forty minutes, something like that. The California went out with a Lieutenant Commander in command. My captain was on board, but I recollect that the navigator was ashore.

We were all steamed up about this, and it was not until we had cleared the harbor and formed up outside that we were told that this was a drill. There was nothing to indicate that it was a drill at all. Everybody was at general quarters. The guns were manned! The powder was up. It was a stimulating, stirring time. I think he had a lot of guts to do it.

Mr. Mason: What was the reaction to it once they discovered it was merely a drill?

Admiral Johnson: I think all of us felt it was a good exercise. We felt a little let down because we hadn't had any big battle once we got outside.

Mr. Mason: It certainly shattered the routine, didn't it?

Admiral Johnson: It certainly did, and it needed shattering, too, at that time. I've always admired Admiral Reeves very much.

Mr. Mason: He was interested in aviation, too, was he not?

Admiral Johnson: Yes, he was, very interested in aviation. Didn't he command one of the first aircraft carriers?

My assignment in the Tennessee was the assistant gunnery officer the entire time I was on board. I attended Secondary Battery Gunnery School the first year, which was run by another outstanding man, Admiral James Lemuel Holloway, then a Lieutenant Commander.

Mr. Mason: Where was that located?

Admiral Johnson: That was aboard the California that I attended this gunnery school. All the assistant gunnery officers in the fleet and the secondary battery officers in the fleet were on board. As I remember it was about six weeks. We did a tremendous lot of firing. We all got so used to firing that it was no great strain any more. We didn't get taut and tense when the time came for us to fire the guns.

It was such a privilege for me to attend this because the second summer I was made the Commander of the Gunnery School myself, the Director of the Gunnery School that was operated at sea. So the experience of the year before was very helpful. We learned a great deal from that.

Mr. Mason: You had gunnery contests, did you?

Admiral Johnson: Yes. You get a score in each practice, and that score is related to the scores of the other ships. I'm very proud to say that my secondary battery had the amazing record - in short range battery practice there were one hundred shots and they got ninety-six hits. That was because they had had the opportunity of firing so much during the period of the school.

Mr. Mason: What was the system of spotting?

Admiral Johnson: This was short range battle practice only firing at a range of about 17 or 18 hundred yards, and that is just a question of looking through the glasses to see the bullets going to the target. We were just starting airplane spotters at that time.

I remember a message that came in from a spotter for one of the cruisers at that time. The first salvo was fired I think was thirteen or fourteen thousand yards.

I wish I could remember the officer's name - but instead of saying, "Up one hundred right three, or down one hundred," his spot was, "A thing of beauty if a joy forever."

Mr. Mason: Then you had catapult planes.

Admiral Johnson: We had catapult planes in the Tennessee, yes.

Mr. Mason: How many would you carry on the Tennessee?

Admiral Johnson: As I remember if was four. The first time I ever had a catapult shot from the Tennessee it scared me stiff.

Mr. Mason: Who was skipper of the Tennessee?

Admiral Johnson: The skipper was W. W. Smyth, a very fine officer who unfortunately became ill and was transferred to the hospital ship while we were in Panama and died on board that ship. His body was brought back aboard and we went to sea and buried him from the quarterdeck of the Tennessee - a very moving occasion.

Howard H. Benson, later Commodore, was our executive officer and commander of the ship at that time; he succeeded to command, of course.

I remember the day that we took the body out to bury it. All the captains and admirals were coming aboard for this occasion. I was the officer of the deck, and as they came aboard of course they would salute and say, "Permission to come aboard, sir," then they would salute the Captain, who was Benson. Instead of saying, "Good morning Commander, permission to come aboard," they said, "Captain."

Reeves was Commander of the Fleet, and when he came aboard he saluted Benson and said, "Good Morning, Captain." One of my colleagues on board, Lieutenant Pat Parker, leaned over and whispered to me, "He's got it made." And he did become a very distinguished officer.

One other delightful assignment on board -- each officer usually had some athletic assignment on board - to help coach the baseball team or the football team or the basketball team, and I was in charge of one of those. There was very keen sailing competition in the fleet at that time, and I was made the sailing officer of the ship.

That year the Tennessee had done very well indeed in the athletic competitions. The ship that wins the athletic competition is awarded the trophy, which is called "The Iron Man", which they carry for a year, and which is very much coveted by all the battleships. When we got down to the end of the season the outcome of the Iron Man competition really depended upon the last sailing race.

We had on board racing boats which we used in the pulling contests, and we had done quite well in those. But it all came down to the last sailing race, and I am no sailor at all. But we had a young lad named Ellsworth from Maine, an Ensign, who was a great sailor.

I had obtained, on the advice of a sailing friend of mine, Captain Burnes from another ship, the Captain's permission to spend eighteen hundred dollars for a sailing rig to mount in the race boat instead of one of the whale boats - it's so much lighter, but no one had ever thought of sailing them before; this man Byrnes thought that this would work. So we bought this eighteen hundred dollar rig; I think it was actually a six meter rig, and mounted it in the whale boat with Ellsworth in command. We only sailed it at night, practiced with it at night, so that the other ships wouldn't see what we were doing.

The big day came off, and our race boat sailed up to the line to the amazement and consternation of all the rest of the people there.

Mr. Mason: They were all in whalers?

Admiral Johnson: They were all in whalers with very heavy rigs.

Ernie Ellsworth just about left the field; he came in as they rounded the half-way mark. So the Iron Man belonged to the <u>Tennessee</u> for a year.

This enhanced my stature very much in the mind of the Captain, who wanted very much to win the Iron Man - Captain Smyth, but Ellsworth was the one that did it.

Mr. Mason: Did the Fleet engage in any war games?

Admiral Johnson: Yes, they engaged in one war game off Hawaii, a very complicated, extensive one.

Mr. Mason: Against what potential enemy?

Admiral Johnson: Some of our own ships - we had the Blue Fleet and the Red Fleet they called them - just against each other. I think it was the Japanese, of course, that we had had in mind.

Then we had another war game, for two years, in Panama. We transited the Canal in one of them. I don't remember the other war games that we had, possibly one off the California coast.

The Tennessee overhauled twice at Bremerton while I was there. I fell in love with that country.

I held the same job as assistant gunnery officer throughout my three years in the Tennessee.

Mr. Mason: Were you able to observe Admiral Reeves closely during this period with the Pacific Fleet? Admiral Reeves is a most interesting naval figure, I think, and one who doesn't seem to have taken his rightful place in historical records; not much is said about him.

Admiral Johnson: No, I agree. I spoke of this very radical exercise that he had, which is the thing I remember him best by.

I don't know why he hasn't taken his rightful place. I feel that the aviators were not too fond of him themselves; I don't know why that was. Because he was not born and bred an aviator possibly. But I don't think he actually was a pilot of a plane; he just had a period of indoctrination. (Halsey was the same type; Halsey was not an actual pilot.) I don't know why he was not regarded more highly, but I thought he was terrific. But appraisal is largely based on that one exercise.

Mr. Mason: You left the Tennessee after a duty of three years, and returned to Washington . . .

Admiral Johnson: I returned to Washington. While I was aboard the Tennessee in Panama, about two months before I was due to be detached, I received a letter from an officer whom I mentioned earlier, Lieutenant Commander Holloway, who was then in the Office of Naval Operations - I think he was in the Office of Naval Intelligence, which was part of Naval Operations - telling me that a vacancy had arisen in the Mission to Brazil. Actually the Mission had been dormant for some time and was being reconstituted - the whole Mission. And there was a vacancy for a gunnery officer, and would I like to be the gunnery officer for the Mission. I remember I sent him a radio saying, "Affirmative," from Panama. I didn't have time to consult my wife so . . .

Mr. Mason: This meant that you could take her with you?

Admiral Johnson: Yes, I could take her with me.

Shortly after we got back to Long Beach, I was detached and ordered to Washington for a briefing period before going to Brazil. The Mission was just being set up again.

Mr. Mason: What was the purpose of our Mission?

Admiral Johnson: The purpose of the Mission was to teach American professional techniques to the Brazilians. Actually my job was to teach them to shoot their guns, lay out practices for them to fire, write up the instructions and rules under which they would fire, to superintend the firing at their practices, to serve as the gunnery officer on the staff of the Brazilian Commander in Chief, and be available for advice on any gunnery subject.

Mr. Mason: What sort of a navy did they have?

Admiral Johnson: It wasn't very much that they had. They had two cruisers, and about ten destroyers that they had purchased from the British at the end of World War I which were pretty well worn by that time. I think they had two old submarines and a number of auxiliaries, but no aircraft carriers. They had some seaplanes; no planes to be launched from ships, and no carriers at all.

Their navy had been pretty dormant too for the last five or six years since our Mission had been withdrawn. It was being set up again under the leadership of Captain Booth McKinney, with Commander Manahan, known as "Speck" Manahan, as the number two. I was the gunnery officer, there was an engineer, an aviator, I think they had a supply officer - there were about six or seven of us.

So I had six weeks in Washington in ONI, being told what Brazil was all about, what their navy was like, what it needed, what we could give them and sell them, and going to Berlitz School trying to learn Portuguese.

Mr. Mason: Did you succeed in that?

Admiral Johnson: I got to be fairly fluent, but I was terribly ungrammatical. I learned one past, one present, and one future tense, and that's all. I never got into imperfects and genders and all that. But I was quite fluent, and enjoyed it very much.

In fact the day before yesterday I had some Brazilians out at my house for lunch. I was just terribly rusty. They spoke so much better English than I did Portuguese that we did speak mostly English.

We went down, and it was a tremendous experience. I don't know that I learned anything technically at all, but I think we did have them shooting better when we left.

Mr. Mason: That was a mission for teaching was it not? What was the purpose of their fleet, what was their concept of its use?

Admiral Johnson: To guard their country, I think. And to assist their allies if they did have any difficulties with enemy nations. They did participate in World War II, they had a number of ships that sailed with our fleet.

They were wonderful, delightful people. They don't do things like we do . . .

Mr. Mason: What do you mean by that?

Admiral Johnson: They are not very tough on subordinates.

I remember once I had a target practice scheduled for seven o'clock in the morning, which was really too early for the life that they'd been accustomed to. When I went aboard this ship there was hardly anybody up yet. They were supposed to start shooting in fifteen minutes, and they were just starting to stir. This made me furious, so after this I told the Admiral commanding the cruisers about this and that I thought he had to take drastic action. He said he would, and I said, "What action do you propose?" He thought a minute and said, "I'll refuse to invite them to have breakfast with me." That was the punishment.

But they were kind, and delightful, and sympathetic, and wonderful people.

They had some stars in the navy - a man named Ayres da Fonseca Costa, who was in charge of their shore ordnance installations - he would have been a hot shot in any navy. He and I got along famously together. We were close friends.

Each one of us had a Brazilian aide assigned to us, and I had a fabulous little man - He was always studying, always delving into things, always asking me questions. I had set down the rules for the gunnery practices, and he had that thing memorized - he was just terrific. He later became the Commander-in-Chief of the Brazilian Navy; he became the first superintendent of their naval academy. He was tough, he would take action, he was a disciplinarian, a delightful man.

I think one of my failures there was I couldn't learn to do the Brazilian Maxixe - a Brazilian dance - which is a beautiful graceful thing, and I couldn't do it. My wife tried to give me lessons, but I didn't succeed in mastering this dance.

Mr. Mason: Where were you based?

Admiral Johnson: Based in Rio. There is a navy department in Rio, in a navy building. The Commander-in-Chief was aboard a ship out in the harbor, but the Chief of Naval Operations' office was in the same building as ours. All the Americans had offices together on the sixth floor.

We went to a place called Ilha a Grande, which was on a beautiful bay. If was fifty miles south of Rio. We went down there for our gunnery exercises. But we were in Rio nine-tenths of the time.

of the time.

They didn't particularly like to go to sea at that time; they had become so accustomed to staying in port in the years that had elapsed since the World War that some of them were very reluctant to go.

Mr. Mason: Admiral, was it a professional man's navy or was it highly political in its complexion and functions?

Admiral Johnson: I think it was pretty professional. They just craved desperately the opportunity to learn to do things. I didn't know of any officers who were deeply involved in politics. Of course, their country was the most political thing you've ever seen - that was one of the difficulties the navy had. The military wasn't much involved in it; it was civilian politics.

I lived in a lovely place on Aveneda Viera Souto, which was on the sea, in the section of the town called Ipahema and I had just to walk across the street to be on the most beautiful beach that you've ever seen. The time of the carnival is something that you remember for ever and for ever - this is Holy Week. For a week then the town goes crazy, everybody dances all the time, goes around in costumes; it's a terrific celebration. I don't know how holy it is; it seems to be mostly fun.

I thoroughly enjoyed that time. I don't know whether it helped me professionally very much, but I think it's helped me in getting along with foreigners. I later received a decoration from the Brazilians in Washington.

Mr. Mason: Yes, in terms of fostering your own career it was a tangent, wasn't it?

Admiral Johnson: Yes, that's right, it was a tangent. And some people thought I was making a mistake to be down there; that I was out of the main stream. But now I wouldn't take anything for having gone.

One of my shipmates there, the aviator in the Mission, became a very distinguished naval aviator, Admiral Edward C. Ewing. He was a famous football player, and captain of the navy football team.

Mr. Mason: What were his duties? They didn't have carriers, they didn't have planes on ships.

Admiral Johnson: They didn't have planes on ships, but he was teaching them how to fly the seaplanes that they had.

Mr. Mason: Were they American origin, or British?

Admiral Johnson: They were American origin. They had some smaller planes, too, something like our battleship planes, that they flew from the water. I flew back and forth to Ilha a Grande a number of times.

Mr. Mason: They were little observation planes, were they?

Admiral Johnson: Yes, observation planes, just a two-seater, one seat behind the other. I was never too happy flying around in them, but we always made it, and never ran out of gas.

Mr. Mason: Did we have other naval missions in Latin America at that time?

Admiral Johnson: We had one in the Argentine, a much smaller one. There were only three officers there. In Chile we had either two or three officers, and in Peru we had one. But I had no association with any of these.

Mr. Mason: Who instigated the sending of the Naval Mission - was it a request from the Latin State?

Admiral Johnson: I think it was a request from the Latin State.

Mr. Mason: And we were happy to comply?

Admiral Johnson: Oh yes, we were. It gave us an in with them, because it helped us to make friends with their country, to put them on our side when the war came; it was a good thing to do.

Mr. Mason: And not too much expense involved in it.

Admiral Johnson: No, very small expense.

Mr. Mason: Were they good at maintaining their ships?

Admiral Johnson: No, not very, no. That was the engineer's biggest job. His biggest job, I think, was to teach them proper maintenance.

It was quite a problem. They had one battleship - the Sao Paulo - and it was quite a problem getting the big guns to operate. Of course, they had them operating on a terribly restricted budget, and it costs a hell of a lot to fire one of those guns. I think those battleship guns - it probably cost a thousand dollars every time they were fired.

While I was there I had saved up a little money. It was a great advantage - you're paid by both the navies. Not very much by the foreign navy - I think I got two hundred or two hundred and fifty dollars a month from the Brazilian Navy, and the regular pay from the American Navy.

This was the first time that I had really been financially comfortable since I'd graduated from the Naval Academy. So when the time came to come home -- I'd always wanted to go to England and Scotland so we had booked passage to England in a freighter from Rio. My wife and I had this all planned out; we were taking the children with us - I had my two daughters with me there.

And at that time the war clouds were brewing in Europe, and I received a dispatch from later Admiral Russell Wilson, with whom I had later relationships, too. He was our attache in London. He said, "By no means bring your family to England at this time."

Mason: In '38?

Admiral Johnson: In '38. So we came home in the freighter anyway, and it was a delightful trip - from Santos to New York in this freighter.

Mr. Mason: It must have been pleasant for your family.

Admiral Johnson: Oh, it was.

Mr. Mason: What kind of living quarters did you have (in Brazil)?

Admiral Johnson: We had two excellent houses. I lived first for a year in the house of the manager of the German bank who was going home for a year - I rented the house from him. And then I rented another very nice house.

We had a delightful Ambassador there - Hugh Gibson - a very accomplished man. Mr. Gibson was the Ambassador when we first arrived and for about six months after we were there.

I was told that he was responsible for the Gibson cocktail - this is as you know, a martini with an onion in it instead of an olive. The origin of that is that Mr. Gibson became ill and was forbidden to take any alcohol, but he still had to have his big dinners at the Embassy. And to keep it from being apparent that he was not drinking he had something that looked like a martini made - it was just water - with an onion in it instead of an olive, so that he could pick the right one from the tray when it was brought around. It was amusing - that belonged to Mr. Gibson, so that became the Gibson cocktail. I later crossed in the Queen Mary with him, some years later, and saw he was still drinking the Gibson cocktail.

One little incident I might speak of there - when we came home I brought with me a jangada. It's a raft made of balsa logs on which a sail is mounted, and it's very much used in Brazil by fishermen - probably about the size of this room.

Mr. Mason: Comparable with the Chinese junk, then.

Admiral Johnson: Yes, but it has no superstructure on it at all. It has just a little bench that you sit on, and the mast and the sail.

As my freighter passed through Bahia on the way home I saw one in the water alongside the ship and asked the Brazilian if he would sell it, and he said he would. I think it cost ten dollars for the whole raft. The captain of the freighter very kindly hoisted it aboard for me and we brought it home. I gave it to the Naval Academy - the Midshipmen use that for playing around with sails. It's probably the only jangada that ever reached America.

Mr. Mason: I wouldn't think it was terribly seaworthy, was it?

Admiral Johnson: You get your feet wet, but it can't sink. You have to have something to hold on to. But they take them one hundred miles to sea.

After my return - we landed in New York and I was met by a messenger of the Navy office with my new orders, which was something which I had requested and had longed for a long time - command of a new destroyer, a new destroyer which was being built at Kearney, New York Shipbuilding Company.

But first I had a months leave, so we went back to Annapolis which was home to us, and had a delightful months leave there.

Then I went up and reported to Kearney where my ship was within about two months of being commissioned. Officers all reported there so we got to know each other.

Mr. Mason: The crew was all selected?

Admiral Johnson: The crew was all selected; I had nothing to do with selecting any of them. They were all over in Brooklyn at the receiving ship.

Finally, I think it was in March, they towed it over to the

Navy Yard in Brooklyn, and the ship was placed in commission with me as it's first captain.

Mr. Mason: Let me ask you - while you were there, several months before she was commissioned, did you have a role in the equipment, in the installation of the equipment or anything of that sort?

Admiral Johnson: I could make suggestions, but they would have to be approved by the inspector in charge, the naval inspector. We did make some few changes. I could point out any shortages that I saw.

But the main thing was getting our crew organized. We spent quite a lot of time with them over in Brooklyn.

Mr. Mason: How large a crew would the Lang carry?

Admiral Johnson: It was about two hundred and twenty. I drew a very superior crew and a wonderful group of officers.

We commissioned her in Brooklyn, and sailed on our shakedown cruiser shortly thereafter.

Mr. Mason: Now what sort of ordnance did she have which was brand new?

Admiral Johnson: She had four five-inch guns, dual purpose

guns, and anti-aircraft - American manufactured. I think she carried twelve torpedoes, and about five or six forty-millimeter guns (or possibly it was twenty millimeters, I can't remember).

We commissioned in Brooklyn, and we had about a month after that to get her ready and then we sailed.

Mr. Mason: Did she have any special protection against submarines?

Admiral Johnson: No, if a submarine hit you, you'd be gone. But she carried depth charges - we could use offensive weapons against them.

We finally sailed. A chief quartermaster named Williams was the helmsman - he had the wheel going out of the harbor. We took a pilot to the entrance of the Brooklyn Navy Yard and dropped him off there.

My first ship, my first command, I was under some tension. We headed down the channel past Governor's Island, when it seemed to me things began to whistle by rather fast, and Williams, the quartermaster, said, "Captain, I'm having difficulty steering."

We looked up, and the starboard engine was going ten knots, which was what I had rung up; the port engine was making twenty-two knots - the first time underway. This was lack of experience of the throttle man, who did not know that something called the "throttle by-pass" had to be open so that when you rolled the throttle open you could bring it back. If you had the throttle by-pass closed when you roll the throttle you can't get it back. So he had rolled it over to twenty to get started and bring it back, only he couldn't bring it back.

Mr. Mason: And he hadn't reported this . . .

Admiral Johnson: The engine room called up just at that time.

So we went out of the harbor with about twenty-two knots on one engine and ten knots on the other. Williams, bless him, steering with a lot of rudder on one side, which, of course, could compensate for that. We were going much faster than you are allowed to go in New York harbor. We went by tugs that were screaming at us and blowing whistles at us, but we didn't get it fixed until we got down past Governor's Island. We hadn't hit anything and we breathed a sigh of relief and thought we could relax.

Mr. Mason: Like an automobile almost out of control.

Admiral Johnson: Like an automobile almost out of control - an automobile that you can't stop, you can't slow down -- that's what it was.

So that was my beginning . . .

Mr. Mason: That must have been a frightening experience.

Admiral Johnson: It was.

We went down to Guantanamo then, to New Orleans - a delightful experience, and Galveston.

Mr. Mason: After that experience, did it cause you to instigate many many more drills?

Admiral Johnson: Yes, we had a great many more drills, but I think it was a help to me in giving me more confidence in meeting an emergency. And it gave the crew confidence, too, that we had been able to handle this; it made us feel that we could handle future difficulties.

And then we came back. After a shakedown cruise you pass a readiness inspection down at Norfolk by the group of inspectors there. They went over us with a fine tooth comb, and put us through the exercises -- we passed that.

Then we went back to get ready to join the fleet. We had about three weeks in New York to get ready, when I was told to come down to Washington. I went down to see this officer in the Chief of Naval Operations' office. He said, "You're going to have a very confidential mission, and that is to accompany the President on a cruise. It will be your task to take him on board, take him out and put him on a cruiser, and escort the cruiser wherever she goes, and then to land him wherever he wants to land." This was President Roosevelt - this was the first time I'd ever seen him.

He was to embark in New York, so I left the Brooklyn Navy Yard and went around to the North River and tied up to a dock in the North River. The President came on board . . .

Mr. Mason: You hadn't been able to advise your crew, had you?

Admiral Johnson: Not until the morning we sailed. They knew something unusual was happening, and I had confided in my officers, because they had to build a ramp on board. It takes a special ship to handle the President.

Mr. Mason: Later on this became recognized quite readily.

Admiral Johnson: It was common knowledge after that, yes.
We built this ramp from the gangway up to the upper deck where the cabins were located, and also we had to put handrails throughout the part of the ship that he might use. The shower had to be cut down so he didn't have to step over. We got all that fixed up.
He came on board - he was only on board long enough for me to take him out to put him aboard the Tuscaloosa. I went alongside the Tuscaloosa.

Mr. Mason: Where was she?

Admiral Johnson: Anchored out in the stream - the Hudson River.

I remember at that time the feeling of fondness for photographers, some of which I have to some degree lost since then (news photographers). When he got out of his car, they had to pull his trousers up above his knee to fasten the braces - the photographers were all around, but no photographer took a picture of that, which I felt was pretty decent. I believe now that some of them would be taking pictures throughout the whole thing.

The President's only mission, to the best of my knowledge, was to get away from it all, have a rest, a sea voyage, do some fishing. On the way up we went into the port in Canada, the name of which I cannot remember now.

Mr. Mason: Did he stop at Campobello, that's in the Bay of Fundy?

Admiral Johnson: We stopped at Campobello, but he did not go ashore. Then we went into a Canadian port, the name of which I cannot remember. The President's flag was flying from the Tuscaloosa. They had been alerted to the fact that he was coming in, so all the state and city officials came on board to call on him as soon as he got there, and, of course, I went over. Every time the Tuscaloosa anchored I went over for any orders he had for me.

Mr. Mason: It was just the one destroyer with the cruiser?

Admiral Johnson: Just the one destroyer.

The President told them how happy he was to be up in Canada; he had always loved Canada. He said the only reason he came in at this time was that he had a great yearning for lobster. You could see them all look at each other in consternation. He said, "What's the matter?" They said, "Well, sir, this is not the lobster season. The lobster season doesn't open until two weeks from now."

He said, "My God, here I've come all the way in here one hundred miles out of my way to get lobster, and you haven't got any lobsters." They put their heads together and said, "Well, sir, if you can stay until tomorrow afternoon we could get some by raiding some illegal pots around here."

The President said, "No, I'm sorry, I've got to leave this afternoon. I'd like to have them today. I'll tell you -- I'll leave Johnson here with the destroyer, and you give him the lobsters. He'll bring them up to me in the Bay of Islands tomorrow."

Then he shook his finger at me and said, "And I want them for dinner, you understand?"

The next morning early they brought I think it was about six or eight dozen lobsters on board my ship, and I took off in the *Lang* - that was my destroyer, USS *Lang* #399 - and we had to average something like twenty-eight knots the whole day to get there by dinner. (He was in the Bay of Islands on the west coast.) We went alongside about a quarter of six and delivered the lobsters. The President gave me a bit of praise and a dozen lobsters, so he had his lobsters, and we had ours.

Then we came back to New York (this was in '39) and he wanted to be dropped off at Fort Totten down in Sandy Hook. So the Tuscaloosa anchored two or three miles out and I went alongside and took him off and went in and made a landing alongside the dock - put him off there. He was kind enough to give us a photograph and to speak to the crew as he left - a great occasion.

Then we went back to New York and had some gunnery exercises. When we were just ready to go to the Pacific to join the fleet, I was called down to Washington again. They said, "The President wants to go on another cruise."

Mr. Mason: And he'd asked for you?

Admiral Johnson: I don't know whether he did or not; I could never get the Navy to say that, but I hope that was right.

They said this was especially secretive this time so they didn't want the ramp put on in any United States port; I should go to Guantanamo and have all the alterations made, and then go to Pensacola and pick the President up there. So I did go to Guantanamo and had another destroyer with me, a destroyer called the Jouett, but the Jouett was not fitted to handle him; it was just an escort. So I took him on board at Pensacola and put him aboard the Tuscaloosa.

That time was a great crisis, because just as I backed away from the dock the Tuscaloosa anchored out in the harbor began to swing to the tide. So I tried to catch the ship when it was swinging, and I didn't do a very smooth operation, but I did get alongside. It probably took about ten or fifteen minutes longer than it should have, and most civilians I think would have been very impatient about it, and when I went down to see the President leave the ship he said, "Captain, don't you feel badly about that landing. I think you did damn well to make it at all." So he was a seaman and he appreciated the difficulty that I had.

We followed him to Panama, and through the Canal, and down to the Cocos Islands, which I suppose are two or three hundred miles from Panama or something like that.

He just wanted to go fishing, but he gave me a job while he was there to make a survey of the harbor, and I did that.

We transited the Canal again, and went back to Pensacola. This was quite a crisis in our lives, too, because we arrived off of Pensacola in a dense fog. The Tuscaloosa couldn't go in the harbor; we had to anchor outside.

To my amazement I got a radio saying, "Come alongside," in the dense fog. They rang and rang and rang the bell - rang it steadily - and told me the heading that they were on. And I got on the reverse of that heading, and came up very slowly. When I got within fifty yards of it I could see it, so we got alongside and took him on board.

Mr. Mason: He wouldn't wait?

Admiral Johnson: No, he was in a hurry to get back to Washington; he had some kind of a crisis in Washington.

He never went below; he sat down on the forecastle under the bridge of the destroyer in a chair, on a short run like that. We started in, it was still foggy. I was making ten knots. He beckoned to me to come down to the forecastle and he said, "Is that all the speed this bucket can make?" I said, "No sir." He said, "I'm in a hurry, get on in there." So I went back and held my breath and cranked up fifteen knots, and we got inside the harbor and then the fog cleared.

But then he beckoned for me to come down again and said, "Have you ever made this dock before?" I said, "No, I made one adjacent to it, but not this one." He said, "Well, this is a hard dock to make. The last time I came in here in a destroyer the captain came in too slowly, let his bow get jammed up alongside one dock and his stern against the other, and I don't want that to happen again. You understand?" - our Commander-in-Chief!

So I bit my fingernails and went up on the bridge, screwed up my nerve, and came in roaring because there was a full ebb tide running across the face of the dock. I warned the chief engineer to have everybody stand by. As we passed the end of the dock we backed emergency for everything and it docked just beautifully in the right place. If we hadn't backed that way we'd have knocked the hell off the bow, of course. But it stopped at the right place; the Lord was with me. He thought that was fine; he left us and that was the last time I saw him.

However, on the way in I had told him that my ship was to sail to join the Pacific Fleet just as soon as it got back and took off the gear, and I was afraid I was going to miss this problem if I could only make fifteen knots. So he turned to his naval aide and said, "Write him a signal giving him permission to make twenty-five knots."

So we went back to Norfolk and unloaded our gear and sailed for the Pacific.

Mr. Mason: May I ask - you said he gave you a task to go out and survey the Cocos Islands - did you know why, what was the purpose?

Admiral Johnson: Yes, he spoke of it. He thought it might be a place, if we ever had a war with Japan, where we might want to establish a base.

Mr. Mason: You said the President had two aides with him . . .

Admiral Johnson: The two aides were General Watson of the Army and Admiral Callahan of the Navy. Admiral Callahan was later killed at Guadalcanal. He was a wonderful man and seemed very close to the President, as did General Pa Watson.

Possibly an amusing story about Pa Watson is that the ships were dry, of course - no liquor was served. I don't know what went on in the President's cabin, but no liquor was served in the Navy part of the Tuscaloosa. General Watson put a sign up over his door - Fort Watson, and said that Navy rules did not hold on an Army reservation. What went on inside, I don't know.

Mr. Mason: I think the President wore his Army hat, too.

Admiral Johnson: I think he wore his Army hat, yes.

Mr. Mason: Why did he select the Tuscaloosa?

Admiral Johnson: I guess she was just available.

The Lang then had orders to sail to the Pacific to join the Pacific Fleet. We transited the Canal, and went up to San Diego. I think we only had two days in San Diego before the Fleet sailed from the West Coast to a problem off Pearl Harbor. The Lang joined up with this parent organization.

I've forgotten the number of the destroyer division now, but it was commanded by one of the Navy stars, Admiral A. S. Merrill, Captain Tip Merrill. I wish you had a record of his recollections.

Mr. Mason: And the Fleet was under the command of J. O. Richardson.

Admiral Johnson: J. O. Richardson, who also was a simply wonderful man. Admiral Richardson was the one who had permitted me to leave the Navy temporarily to make the yachting trip; he was the assistant Chief of Personnel at that time. Very few people would have had the understanding that he had.

We went through the operations, and learned a lot from it.

Mr. Mason: Now this was a protective thing for the Hawaiian Islands?

Admiral Johnson: Yes, it was a protective operation.

Mr. Mason: Was there anything in these war games that would have been useful in the time of the actual attack?

Admiral Johnson: I'm afraid I had such a worms eye view of the operations in those days that I just am not qualified to say, but I don't believe we had any Japanese observing us during this operation. At least I don't know of any. And it was awfully good for us all to have the experience of going into and out of Pearl Harbor - learning the geography and topography there.

I remember one night there -- another one whom I'm very fond of took me back to the Lang one night in his barge, Frank Jack Fletcher. I remember his telling me of the many mistakes he'd made in the Navy; one mistake he had _not_ made was failing to buy a farm. He told me he had a farm in Southern Maryland; that's the first time I think that I ever thought of owning a farm in Southern Maryland. I have visited him at his farm, near Waldorf. He's a very ill old man, and spends a great deal of time at Bethesda. The name of his farm is Araby.

Upon the conclusion of the operations off Pearl Harbor I was ordered to accompany the cruiser _Philadelphia_ from Pearl to Bremerton. I think they must have been a little nervous in these days because they would not send their cruisers off alone - I had no mission in Bremerton myself; it was just to go up and escort the _Philadelphia_ up there. I think they must have felt a little nervous about letting any ship go to sea.

Mr. Mason: That was not a peace time precaution.

Admiral Johnson: No, I don't think it was.

So we took the _Philadelphia_ up, dropped her at Bremerton, spent about one day there, and then returned to San Diego or San Pedro - I'm not sure which.

Vice Admiral Felix L. Johnson   Interview #3
Leonardtown, Maryland
November 2, 1971
By: John T. Mason, Jr.

Mr. Mason: As usual, it's a great pleasure to see you today, sir.

Admiral Johnson: Thank you, doctor, it's wonderful to have you back at Jubilee again.

Mr. Mason: Last time you concluded by saying that in command of the Lang you escorted the Philadelphia to Bremerton. How long did you stay at Bremerton, and what was the situation at the naval yard there on that occasion?

Admiral Johnson: We only stayed one day there, and after that I was ordered to San Diego, which was the normal United States base for the Lang. The situation did not seem to be abnormal as far as I could see, except that I was impressed by the fact that this cruiser did have to have an escort in crossing the Pacific from Hawaii. We went along from Bremerton down to San Diego, and after a very short time in San Diego for replacement of some ammunition, and I think we changed some of our crew, we went back to Pearl again.

Mr. Mason: Did you have a full complement on the Lang - a war time complement?

Admiral Johnson: No, not quite as much as we had later, but a full peace time complement. I've forgotten which is a complement and which is an allowance; I think it's a peace time allowance and a war time complement - they use these expressions.

Mr. Mason: In terms of personnel what did the Lang carry?

Admiral Johnson: I think I carried about one hundred and ninety people at that time.

I was detached from the Lang very shortly after she arrived in Pearl - I took her back to Pearl and was detached there - and ordered to commission and command the Castor. It was a merchant ship, and really what the Navy called a "beef boat" in those days. That's a supply ship. It's maybe a little term of contempt for the beef boat as opposed to the fighting ship.

So I was ordered to command the Castor, which was first a ship called the SS Challenge, which the Navy had bought and was converting to what is called a "general stores issue ship." A general stores issue ship is something like a floating hardware store, and we carried something like, I think, fifteen thousand items on board. Our task was to accompany the Fleet wherever it went, and be ready to issue to them any part or material which they needed for the maintenance and upkeep of the ships.

Mr. Mason: And for minor repairs?

Admiral Johnson: No, we made no repairs, just purely to issue.

This was an interesting experience for me because I was the only regular naval officer on the ship; all the rest of them were reserves. And just at this time we were beginning to order reserve divisions back to duty. We had one entire reserve division, as I recall, from a place called Kingston, New York. I had about one hundred and ten aboard, and something like sixty of those came together from this reserve division in Kingston.

We commissioned the ship again in New York, and loaded her with all kinds of equipment that really was a strange looking sight when we sailed from New York. We had a big tug sitting up on the bow, and we were taking twenty or thirty automobiles out to Pearl - they were stacked all over the decks. Finally when we sailed from Norfolk we were towing a huge barge astern. This was a very complicated thing.

Mr. Mason: What was her normal speed?

Admiral Johnson: About twelve or thirteen knots.

Mr. Mason: When she was intended to accompany the Fleet?

Admiral Johnson: She would just rendevouz with the Fleet in its various anchorages; it did not accompany them when they were actually underway, but was present at the anchorages to issue to them whatever they needed.

Mr. Mason: Was she then part of what came to be known as the "supply train?"

Admiral Johnson: Yes, she was.

We dropped off our barge at Guantanamo, and then sailed to Panama and through the Canal, and straight from there out to Pearl.

One thing I was very pleased with - the commander of the train out there was so impressed with how much stuff we had on deck that he sent a photographer down to take a picture of it. He said he wanted people to know how much a ship could carry. And that was a great satisfaction.

Mr. Mason: This idea of a fleet train was something of an innovation, wasn't it?

Admiral Johnson: No, we had had that for some time, but they had not had a general stores issue ship. They had had repair ships in there, and supply ships, that carried some of the things, but no one ship which carried these thousands of parts -- this was an innovation at that time.

I was only in this ship for a very short while out there, I think something like four or five months after we got to Pearl, when I was detached and ordered to the Naval Academy.

Mr. Mason: And before you tell me about that sir, would you discourse a bit on the reserve officers in the Navy, since the Challenge was manned largely by reserve officers?

Admiral Johnson: She was manned almost entirely by reserves, and they were simply splendid. A number of them were merchant marine reserves; most of them were the organized reserve.

I would like to talk in considerable length about the reserves later, because since I've retired I have three times been ordered back to active duty as chairman of boards to look into the reserve and see what should be done about it. I have some very strong convictions.

Mr. Mason: Splendid, I shall look forward to that.

Admiral Johnson: So I was detached and ordered to the Naval Academy as what is called Aide to the Superintendent and Secretary of the Academic Board.

Mr. Mason: Was this an assignment which you looked forward to? Did you know that you were going to be sent there?

Admiral Johnson: No, I didn't know it. I was very pleased. I think it was a coveted assignment, and I was delighted to be there with a most wonderful Superintendent, at that time Vice Admiral Russell Wilson.

This Secretary of the Academic Board is in effect the Director of Admissions - that's his function -- to decide who is acceptable to the Navy for entrance into the Naval Academy and who is not, to administer their examinations, to keep the records, to arrange the physical examinations. It was sometimes something of a cruel job - when you had to tell someone that he hadn't made it. But again there were lots of times when you could tell him he had.

A simply delightful assignment - I thoroughly enjoyed it. I had very close association with the Superintendent; I had the office next to him. You are his senior aide and travel with him.

I think I reported there in August or September, and I was there, of course, when the war started.

Mr. Mason: Would you tell me, sir, in more detail about this job? It had many ramifications, I'm sure, as you sketched. You got involved with members of Congress undoubtedly?

Admiral Johnson: A great deal of involvement with members of Congress, and with civilian educational institutions - with the presidents and deans of admissions of any number of colleges.

Mr. Mason: Can you cite any instances?

Admiral Johnson: The one that I treasure the most possibly was with Phinney Baxter, the President of Williams. I met him when he came down to the Naval Academy to talk to the Midshipmen.

We tried to have, about once a month, some distinguished civilian who came and talked to the Midshipmen. And also about once a month we tried to have a distinguished churchman who preached in Chapel to the Midshipmen.

I got to know Dr. Baxter when he came down, and later I was to become a member of the Holloway Board with him - the board which established the system of education for young reserves after the war. He's a simply wonderful man.

Dr. Seymour of Yale was another one that I met at that time. I'm afraid I can't remember all the others.

Mr. Mason: You worked with these men - so many of the applicants to the Naval Academy came from these universities . . .

Admiral Johnson: Were enrolled in these universities, yes.

Mr. Mason: What was the maximum age limit for entry?

Admiral Johnson: Entry was nineteen. You could enter at nineteen at that time; you could not when you reached twenty. I believe it's one year older at this time.

They would submit the records of these young men to us. We would go over them and tell them wherein he was short, what he needed to take, and what he could do to qualify. There were several means of admission - you could enter with a college certificate without any examination at all, or you could take some substantiating examination in about two subjects and be accepted on your record on the other subjects, or you could take a straight examination across the board.

Mr. Mason: And these straight examinations were conducted by the Civil Service Commission, were they?

Admiral Johnson: Yes, they were arranged by the Naval Academy, but they were given by the Civil Service. We turned the examinations over to them; they administered the examination for us all in one day, all over the United States.

Mr. Mason: Were you involved also with some of the prep schools?

Admiral Johnson: Many of them, more than colleges really, because it was while a lad was in prep school that the idea usually came to him that he wanted to go to the Naval Academy. The head of the school would communicate with us at the Naval Academy.

My favorite there, if I can say I had one, is Dr. Boyden of Deerfield. He was a most wonderful man. My meeting with

Johnson #3 - 120

him was a rather strange thing. We'd keep a record of what the product of every school in the United States does at the Naval Academy. We'd get them altogether - everyone from Harvard, everyone from Exeter, everyone from Andover, everyone from Deerfield. I was looking over the Deerfield records one day; they only had as I remember nineteen lads from Deerfield that had entered the Naval Academy and all of them but one had starred there. A star is equivalent of Phi Beta Kappa, 3.4 - making 3.4 in everything. Every boy but one from Deerfield had starred. I was so impressed with that that I wrote a letter to Dr. Boyden, whom I'd never met at that time, and told him what the record was. I thought that was something to be proud of. We got to be close friends after that; he came down and visited us - he was a simply wonderful man.

Mr. Mason: I suppose, sir, there was a correlation between the interest of the head of the school like that in the Naval Academy and the number of boys who came.

Admiral Johnson: There was indeed, yes. They would so often guide a lad who was somewhat at a loss as to what he was going to do next. They'd ask him if he'd thought of the Naval Academy, or if he thought of West Point. They'd give him the guidance and prepare him for that.

Mr. Mason: Being aware of that sir, did you do some missionary

Johnson #3 - 121

work with schools that didn't have a record with the Naval Academy?

Admiral Johnson: I think we tried to get retired officers who lived in communities to go to the high schools in their communities and arrange to make a talk on the Naval Academy to the senior class. We had a great many who did that, and we had quite a number of reserve officers who did that for us, too.

Mr. Mason: Did you have literature to supply them with?

Admiral Johnson: Yes.

We now have officers called "Blue and Gold" officers, and that is, I think, their main mission in life - to guide and help select the young men to enter the Navy. I don't know whether it's all just Naval Academy or to enter through other means, too. I'm sure that's based at the Academy - this Blue and Gold movement.

Mr. Mason: They come for a two or three week training period, a refresher.

Did you have on occasion - did you have political pressure applied on you to admit boys whom Congressmen were especially interested in?

Admiral Johnson: Yes, but never successfully, I'm proud to say.

Mr. Mason: How did you withstand it?

Admiral Johnson: By just explaining the standards of the Academy, and that we could not make exceptions for anyone. And we were sure that their young man was a fine young man but he didn't have such and such credentials, and if he took these courses he could qualify. We tried always to give them means of qualifying.

But it wasn't very bad; there were a few Congressman who got nasty about it. But the Superintendent was adamant that we should never knuckle under any kind of pressure at all, and there wasn't very much of it.

Mr. Mason: What about the boys who came in by Presidential appointment -- were they very numerous at that time?

Admiral Johnson: Yes. As I remember it we allowed fifty Presidential appointments, and something like fifty or seventy-five from the fleet. But, of course, he had to qualify academically just the same as anybody else has to - this assures him an appointment. Any son of an officer or an enlisted man can take a competitive examination for Presidential appointment, and the top fifty get it if they have the other qualifications necessary to enter.

Mr. Mason: Aren't there some special schools maintained by the

Johnson #3 - 123

Navy . . .

Admiral Johnson: Yes, there's one at Bainbridge. This would be a lad who would be nominated for this assignment by his commanding officer, and if the Navy accepted this nomination, they would send him to Bainbridge to the Naval Academy Preparatory School, where he had a year to prepare for the examinations for entry. This was to help out the sailor.

Mr. Mason: What relationship did you have with a school like that?

Admiral Johnson: None, except to advise them as to the necessary requirements for entry. I think I went to Bainbridge once or twice to consult with the officer who was in charge of the school. I had no power there, no influence at all.

Mr. Mason: How did you arrive at the number of men to be admitted on a given occasion?

Admiral Johnson: It was increasing quite rapidly at that time. Back in my entry of 1916 that was the largest class that had ever entered; it was five hundred and twenty, I think. It had grown through the years until when I went back to this job it was something like a thousand that they were taking. This was based on the needs of the Navy, how many officers were required.

It's now standardized at about thirteen hundred and fifty that enter each year, but, I believe they get a much bigger selectivity than they used to. I think a lot more lads know about the Naval Academy. This work of the Blue and Gold officers has had its effect.

Mr. Mason: What was the attrition rate in this time when you were there, before the war?

Admiral Johnson: As I remember it, it was roughly thirty percent.

Mr. Mason: Has that been fairly stable through the years?

Admiral Johnson: When the war came it slacked off a bit. I think we needed them so badly probably that we kept some that we might not have kept before. I think it got down to eighteen percent at one time, and I think I've seen that at one time since the war that it was forty percent. I think it probably runs about twenty or thirty now.

Mr. Mason: What was the prevailing attitude in the country at large towards service in the military prior to World War II?

Admiral Johnson: It was warming up all the time. People were beginning to see the war clouds on the horizon and, God bless them, a great many of them wanted to have a part in it if we were so unfortunate to have this come to us.

I'll tell a little incident - When I was commissioning the Castor, I went back to the Navy yard one night and stopped by the New York Yacht Club, which I had joined three or four years before and very seldom had entered.

At that time we were trying out a kind of promotion in the Navy - they selected officers from the top list that they called "best fitted." Then they would select a second group called "fitted." That was the first year it was tried.

I went down in the bar at the New York Yacht Club and sat down by myself over in the corner; I was alone. There were twelve men, none of whom I'd ever seen before, sitting at a big table over in the middle of the bar - great friends having a good time. One of them came over and asked me if I wouldn't join them, and I did. They introduced themselves and I said, "I'm Commander Felix Johnson."

He said, "Are you Lieutenant Commander or Commander?" I said, "Commander." He said, "Oh, Commander, fitted or best fitted?" I said, "Well, as a matter of fact, I'm best fitted." And as one man they rose to their feet and raised their glasses, and said, "We've never met a best fitted Commander before, welcome to the club." This just showed the interest.

During the war I think I saw at least ten of those twelve

in uniform; the New York Yacht Club just solidly went to the Navy.

But this was an indication of the way people were beginning to think about us. Recruitment was very easy; I think everybody on Long Island went in the Navy.

Remember when I spoke of my sailing race to Spain - I really believe that every single person in that race went in the Navy. I didn't know any of them who didn't, and they brought their boats with them.

That brings me up to the beginning of the war . . .

Mr. Mason: There must be other aspects of this job at the Academy that you want to talk about, however. Since you were involved with recruitment and so forth, you must have inadvertently been involved with accommodations and all that.

Admiral Johnson: One thing I was involved with -- We had the Board of Visitors made up of distinguished educators at that time. As I remember there were about fourteen or fifteen. And that met - twice while I was there - the Secretary of the Academic Board is the Secretary of the Board of Visitors, so I had a great deal to do with them. That's where I met many of my educator friends, who proved to be of such wonderful assistance to me later.

Mr. Mason: When the Board comes to the Academy what are they exposed to? What is the routine?

Admiral Johnson: As I remember it we'd meet together with the Superintendent, the Commandant, and the heads of the departments in the Naval Academy. The Superintendent would make a talk of welcome to them, and tell them everything was open to them. And they then broke up into sub-committees -- a sub-committee being assigned to each department -- and they went to that department and spent several days looking into the courses there.

Mr. Mason: Did they live on campus?

Admiral Johnson: I think they were taken in the houses of the senior officers there; I had a couple of them staying with me. I think all the rest of them did stay in the houses of the captains.

At the end of that period there they submitted a report to the Superintendent telling him the good things they'd found, and the bad things they'd found, and places where they thought improvement could be made. The Superintendent usually would listen very carefully to what they advised him, because there were tremendous men among them. I remember Dr. Frank Graham of the University of Carolina was one.

Mr. Mason: Colgate Darden was a member of the Board while you were there, wasn't he?

Admiral Johnson: Colgate Darden was terrific, he was just the best.

I always think of Frank Graham though -- when working with education when I was with the Bureau of Personnel, we would have to get educators to appear before the Naval Affairs Committee to testify for what we were trying to accomplish. We had Dr. Seymour of Yale down. Mr. Vinson, the Chairman from Georgia, was always very cool to these gentleman if they talked with a yankee accent when they appeared before him. He was a tremendous friend of the Navy and a wonderful man.

I remember once we were in a terrible bind over the ROTC program and we weren't getting our way with it. Somebody suggested we get Dr. Frank Graham to come up. He entered and sat down. Just as soon as Mr. Vinson heard his North Carolina accent he said, "Mr. President, I'm so happy to have you here, you just sit down and tell me what to do, you all." So we learned to be smarter after that. But Mr. Vinson was simply wonderful, a tremendous friend of the country and the Navy. But that was a later part of my life.

Mr. Mason: Who names the Board of Visitors? Does the Superintendent have a voice in this?

Admiral Johnson: I think not; I think they are named by the Secretary - I'm quite sure they were. I don't know who suggested names to him. I should have looked into that when I was assistant Chief of the Bureau of Personnel, but I don't remember. I probably signed some nominations myself at that time.

This takes up to the first of December.

I said a little while ago it's customary to have distinguished divines come down and talk to the Midshipmen. The man chosen for the 7th of December that year was Peter Marshall. I had never heard of him until then. He was coming from the New York Avenue Presbyterian Church in Washington. He came and preached; he preached the most prescient sermon that one could possibly imagine. The theme was - how short is our tenure of life, or how short is our span of life, and we must be thinking about the long haul instead of just little tiny things. It was a beautiful sermon; you could have just heard a pin drop all over the Chapel. While he was preaching the bombs were falling; it was immediately after Chapel that I got a call telling me about Pearl Harbor.

I spoke to Dr. Marshall about this the next year when he came down - that it was such a remarkably appropriate sermon. He said, "It's a lot stranger than you think. I drove down with my wife and her mother and father that day. About a half hour out of Annapolis something touched me on the shoulder and said, 'You can't use that sermon you've got prepared.' So I turned to them and said, 'Something has told me I can't use the sermon that I was going to give. Will you all please be quiet and let me think of another before we get to Annapolis.'" And he thought up that in a half hour before he got there.

I always thought this was an amazing thing. He was a great man; the best preacher I ever heard. I heard him a number of times in Washington after that.

Of course, this changed lots of things at the Naval Academy. One thing - we speeded up graduation which was due to be the following June. We speeded it up to the 22nd of December - we graduated the first class then. They were in such need of officers.

Mr. Mason: How did the boys respond to the speed-up?

Admiral Johnson: Wonderful - they wanted to go. Some of them wanted to go so badly that they resigned and went out and got a commission as a reserve, just so they could get out instead of having to wait a few months. But most of them stuck it out.

The course was curtailed; we had only three years courses. The course was possibly not quite as difficult as it had been.

Securing competent officers and instructors at the Academy became a very difficult problem. I was the Personnel Officer at the Academy, in addition to being Secretary of the Academic Board, so I had to be constantly in touch with the Detail Office in Washington submitting names that we would like to get, and getting together on whether these people would do or not. We recalled a great many retired officers to active duty, and brought forty or fifty of those to the Naval Academy for duty. This was one of the big problems. This was an older contingent, mostly Lieutenant Commanders and Commanders; I don't think they recalled any Captains at all.

Immediately after Christmas we lost our Superintendent. The U. S. Fleet Command was being established, Admiral King as Commander-in-Chief, and our Superintendent went up to become his Chief of Staff - Admiral Russell Wilson became Admiral Ernest King's Chief of Staff.

Then we got another splendid one - Admiral John Reginald Beardall, a soft spoken, Florida gentleman. He was the Aide to the President before that. I was so blessed, and so was the Academy blessed, to have two such men in this difficult period.

Mr. Mason: At that time what percentage of the teaching staff was civilian?

Admiral Johnson: Much less than it is now. If I remember it, we had something like thirty percent. I think it runs seventy-five to eighty now.

We had some excellent civilians there, but I myself favored keeping this preponderance of the military there because I think the student has got to be absorbing something besides the academic side when he is in the room. And I think it was good for him to sit there with an officer who has just gone through what he is going to go through.

I remember as a Midshipman myself - I tried to pattern

myself on some of the instructors that I admired. And I'm sure that has gone on down through the years.

Mr. Mason: That prompts a question -- what care is exercised in the selection of officer teaching personnel? Not every man is equipped to teach . . .

Admiral Johnson: Very very little formal supervision.

However, no one is ordered there without his name being acceptable to the Superintendent. The Superintendent can propose to the Bureau that he would like to have Commander John Mason come to the Naval Academy for assignment, and if the Bureau of Personnel can spare him - it depends on how long he's been at sea, whether it fits in with his career pattern. Mostly, though, it's the Bureau proposing officers to the Naval Academy.

And that was one of my jobs - to take that list and go up to Washington and discuss the man with the Detail Officer. And we had permission to look at their records, in sizing them up - whether he was coming or not.

I never knew of them ordering a man there to whom the Superintendent objected. It was not I that made the decision; it was the Superintendent's decision, it was just my recommendation.

In general I think it's always been an accolade to be ordered to the Naval Academy; it was a prize to come.

Mr. Mason: With the outbreak of war did this attitude change? Were some of the men reluctant to come?

Admiral Johnson: Yes, they were, they wanted to go to sea. And that's why we had so many of the retired officers who came back in. I think possibly the percentage of civilians did slowly escalate at the outbreak of the war.

Mr. Mason: Were you able to maintain the same kind of control over selectivity with the retired officers?

Admiral Johnson: Yes.

Mr. Mason: Were some of them in the academic field?

Admiral Johnson: A few were, more of them were in the business world, but a few were in the academic world. Many of them wanted very much to come back to active duty and wrote letters to the Bureau requesting assignment, but not everyone was taken back. All were liable to be called back, but not all were taken back. I think one or two very bad mistakes were made, but in general they were fine and good.

We had a very splendid Commandant, M. S. Tisdale, known as Tip Tisdale. He was a very strong forthright man. He eventually was promoted to Admiral and left just about the time that I did.

I was promoted to Captain in my second year there, and shortly after being promoted to Captain I finally got to go to sea. I was somewhat restless, of course, just sitting there that long - the first year and a half of the war. I was ordered to command a ship called the President Adams, that I'd never heard of.

Mr. Mason: Still, in retrospect, it must have been a very satisfying two years at the Academy.

Admiral Johnson: Oh, it was, it was wonderful - the people that we were associated with there, the interesting people we were meeting. I was beginning to see so many of my yachting friends come through; actually a couple of them were ordered to the Naval Academy as instructors. Many of them were ordered to Washington and would come down and see us. It was just like an old home week every week almost. At Chapel services you'd see people come - people that you hadn't seen in such a long time.

Mr. Mason: It must have been satisfying, too, in a sense that you were in such an influential position to shape the next generation of naval officers.

Admiral Johnson: I don't know how much influence we had, some certainly. It was certainly rewarding to feel that we were having an opportunity to shape the future generation.

Last week I went to a Rotary luncheon in Annapolis and saw two lads who entered while I was the Secretary of the Academic Board - Bill Busick and Dick Duden. Dick Duden was an outstanding athlete and student at Andover; he had been in Andover I think for three years. They took the Naval Academy in a breeze, those two. They were the inspiring type of leaders that you loved to see around.

I saw yesterday something about Vice Admiral I. C. Kidd, who was made Chief of Material in Washington. Ike Kidd graduated in my time. He was the son of the man who was in command of the Nevada at Pearl Harbor, and was killed.

Mr. Mason: Was there any noticable difference between the boys of that pre-World War II era and those whom you had known and were your colleagues in World War I?

Admiral Johnson: I think maybe the latter group was abler, a more outstanding group.

Mr. Mason: You mean - better educational background?

Admiral Johnson: Better educational background, and they had been more carefully chosen, I believe. In the time I came it was rather difficult to get enough people to come to the Academy. I think they took just most anybody that could pass the examination. I had no competition in my district; I was the only one who applied to the Congressman for the appointment.

Mr. Mason: This latter day contingent . . .

Admiral Johnson: There was more competition; I think there was a greater competitive spirit.

Mr. Mason: Did they also reflect changing educational standards in the country?

Admiral Johnson: I expect it did, yes. I'm so old now that if I had to speak of it I'm not sure that I would agree that what's happening in the last few years has been any improvement in educational standards. But I think up until sometime subsequent to the war that they did improve, yes. At least I was so terribly impressed with the caliber of the college men that I met in that period - the administrators, the executors, the deans. I just thought they were a terrific crowd of people.

Mr. Mason: What percentage of your boys coming into the Academy had had college experience actually?

Admiral Johnson: I think it was a little over half, when I was the Secretary of the Academic Board. At the time that I entered I don't believe more than ten or fifteen percent. I had had a half year in college.

Mr. Mason: Since the maximum age for entering was nineteen prior World War II, it would almost mean that there was an element of the precocious, would it not, if the boy had been to the university?

Admiral Johnson: I think that's probably right. If he had been to the university he probably entered at sixteen or seventeen. I entered at seventeen at North Carolina, which had fourteen hundred boys and two girls. Now I understand it has lots of both, something like thirty or thirty-five thousand. And, personally, of course, I liked the small college better; I knew every person on the campus. Certainly I knew the two girls, and it didn't help a bit.

Mr. Mason: Well, you finally broke loose and went to sea.

Admiral Johnson: Yes, went to sea, and was ordered to the President Adams.

Mr. Mason: Was this a command that you rejoiced in?

Admiral Johnson: I rejoiced in it. I think a little of it was the name - the happy association I'd had with the Adams family. I thought it exalted to be in association with them again. I told you, I think, that my skipper in the sailing race was Charles Francis Adams, who later became the Secretary of the Navy. And this was named for his grandfater, President Adams.

The President Adams was what is called an attack transport, one of the Dollar Line Ships that went around the world. It was about eighteen or twenty thousand tons. It carried about six or seven hundred in the crew, and we could carry up to two thousand troops.

Mr. Mason: When had she been commissioned as a naval vessel, after Pearl Harbor?

Admiral Johnson: After Pearl Harbor, yes. She had been commissioned about a year before I took her; she had participated in Guadalcanal for her first operation.

I flew out to the South Pacific to Noumea; that was SoPac Headquarters. That's where my ship was. They said she was down in New Zealand. So a couple of days later I flew down to New Zealand and boarded her there. She was sailing the next morning to go back to Noumea; I rode as a passenger to Noumea, and took command the day after I got back.

And there, also, my crew were all reserves. I don't think I had a single regular on her.

Mr. Mason: What did you say the complement was?

Admiral Johnson: We had somewhere around six or seven hundred men and I think around 65 officers, and I was the only regular. But they were wonderful.

I had one in here for dinner with me last week; he was a sailor on the Azucara in the New York Yacht Club race - Bennett Hammond was my supply officer.

My executive officer was a New York broker, the first lieutenant was a Sears Roebuck salesman, the engineer had been an engineer of a stationary power plant in Southern California. So you see, you get a broad cross-section of America.

Mr. Mason: I would think it would be an interesting group - representing all these different . . .

Admiral Johnson: Very interesting group.

Mr. Mason: Except under wartime conditions you didn't have much chance to share these interests.

Admiral Johnson: You were pretty busy all the time. I remember my navigator was an ROTC lad from Yale, so we did get a great mixture of them. But it was a wonderful experience.

I had a very short cruise in the Adams. I made two or three runs with New Zealanders to Guadalcanal and to New Georgia.

Mr. Mason: May I ask - what was their attitude toward entry into the war and participation?

Admiral Johnson: They seemed very enthusiastic about it; they were deeply committed. The New Zealanders were some of the best people I ever found.

Mr. Mason: Of course, their homeland was being threatened.

Admiral Johnson: It sure was, and so was Australia. Australia had had some bombs dropped in the northwest in Darwin, very very close to them. But the New Zealanders were splendid.

I only made that one trip to New Zealand. I was only there two days I think then; I was wanting to go back. I've been a lot of times in Australia.

After two or three resupply runs, mostly with the New Zealanders to Guadalcanal . . .

Mr. Mason: May I ask what kind of protection you had as a troop carrying ship?

Admiral Johnson: We always had destroyers with us, something like six, and we had air cover sometimes. When we got close in to Japanese-held islands we had air cover.

Mr. Mason: What was the danger from Japanese submarines? Were they rather prevalent in that area?

Admiral Johnson: A couple had been sunk near there, and I think we had had one or two ships sunk of our own. I never saw one the whole time I was out there.

Mr. Mason: You zigzagged, did you?

Admiral Johnson: Yes, we zigzagged all the time.

Mr. Mason: At what speed?

Admiral Johnson: Eighteen knots.

Mr. Mason: How many troops were you carrying?

Admiral Johnson: About two thousand, very crowded it was. We had to feed them all. They had all their own equipment, and their own chaplain - biggest man I've ever seen in my life - Chaplain Burragwanath. He was a New Zealand resident, and very nearly killed on board. I was terribly fond of him.

One day we were having a practice landing. The way they embark in the boats is to go down a cargo net hand over hand to get into the boat, cargo nets strung alongside. He had been ashore and was coming back and apparently was quite tired, and was one of the last to get out of the boat. He climbed and climbed and got almost to the top and he couldn't move further. He hung on, but you could see his hands begin to loosen. The very fast thinking coxswain in the boat gunned his engine and dashed ahead; Burragwanath fell and hit the water just behind the boat. It would have killed him if he'd hit the boat. So he wasn't hurt, just knocked out.

But he was typical of the very splendid people we had.

Mr. Mason: You talk about practice landings - where were these landings conducted?

Admiral Johnson: They were practiced some on Guadalcanal, some in New Georgia . . .

Mr. Mason: Enroute to your destination?

Admiral Johnson: No, this was training periods before we put them ashore in Guadalcanal. Enroute to the destination we made very few landings and then it was just to give them a little exercise.

One day before the Bougainville landing I had eighteen hundred Marines on board. They'd been couped up on board for several days - hot, uncomfortable. So we decided to run over to an island - I've forgotten the name of it now - and we had a practice landing. We landed all eighteen hundred Marines. It was the suggestion of somebody - probably my New York broker -- We sent about fifty cases of beer ashore before the men went ashore, and put them up on the top of a mound in the middle of the island. When they hit the beach they stormed forward and captured the beer, and they all had a couple beers. Then we brought them back on board, and sailed the next day and went through the two fights up there.

A month or so later I was down in Noumea, walking through the hospital grounds, and I met a very tired-looking Marine sergeant - his clothes were all beaten up, he'd been through action. He was sort of drooping along when he saw me; he gave me a very sharp salute and said, "May the sergeant address the Captain, sir?" I said, "Certainly sergeant, what is it?" He said, "The sergeant would like to observe to the Captain that the President Adams is the best damn transport in the South Pacific. It gave the Marines beer before they landed in Bougainville."

Mr. Mason: These were U. S. Marines?

Admiral Johnson: Yes, U. S. Marines.

About the 28th of October we loaded Marines at Espiritu Santo - I believe that we loaded our troops there, possibly some we had picked up down in Noumea. We sailed for Bougainville, Empress Augusta Bay. The landing was to take place in the Bay just inside Cape Torokina.

Mr. Mason: Did you know what you were getting into?

Admiral Johnson: We thought it was going to be worse than it was really, because we had some very effective air cover which was flying from Guadalcanal. The difficulty was that the distance was such that the fighters could only come up and stay about an hour before they had to leave to go back down again, so they had to keep a constant replenishment cover there.

Mr. Mason: They came from Henderson Field, did they?

Admiral Johnson: Henderson Field, yes.

The biggest Jap attack came just as one of these groups of fighters was relieving another one there, so we had twice as many on station as there normally would have been. And that's the first time I ever saw a plane shot down, falling pretty rapidly.

As you see in this picture by Bill Draper, the noted artist, who was in my ship, in the combat art work -- there was an active volcano just back of Empress Augusta Bay. Our landing I think was to be about seven-thirty in the morning, and somewhere around two o'clock that night we steamed toward the Bay. We could see this flame coming from the volcano - quite an eerie thing to see under such circumstances.

Mr. Mason: Were there other troop ships with you?

Admiral Johnson: Yes, there were about five troop ships in there.

Mr. Mason: With what kind of a flotilla?

Admiral Johnson: We probably had about eighteen destroyers. I believe we had one of the light cruisers of the Marblehead class, but just one, nothing heavy at all.

Mr. Mason: Did the President Adams herself have A.A. guns or . . .

Admiral Johnson: Yes, very few, six three-inch fifty caliber.

Mr. Mason: Not a great deal of protection.

Admiral Johnson: No.

I'm glad you asked me that because it was quite a thrill to me when we had reached our spot and anchored, and the lad who was the gunnery officer - I think he was a senior lieutenant reserve - called up to the bridge and asked if he could commence firing.

For the first time in my life I said, "Commence firing" when there was something on the other end firing. He started pumping them out with our little three-inch guns.

We had reached our spot and dropped anchor, and sent our men ashore load after load after load.

But one thing more about that night -- it was the first time in combat for most all of these men and there was some nervousness, of course, and apprehension. I had a wonderful young Baptist chaplain from Texas named Starnes, a junior lieutenant. He had something like twelve hundred men to give communion to that night - he spent the whole night giving communion. I remember his coming up on the bridge about four o'clock and saying, "Captain would you like to have communion? I can give you four minutes worth."

So I have always felt that we could simplify ours in our church because that was the most impressive communion I ever had.

They had a pretty rough time on the beach when they got in. I think I had thirty-one men killed out of those . . .

Mr. Mason: Out of eighteen hundred?

Admiral Johnson: Yes.

They hit the beach, and these planes had straffed the beaches, and had done a lot of good for us before going ashore. So it wasn't nearly as bad as we expected.

To the best of my knowledge my ship was not hit at all. I think a few were hit with small calibers, but that was all.

Mr. Mason: How many of the Zeros came over?

Admiral Johnson: I think at one time I saw eight blazing on

the water; looking around the landscape I saw eight planes on fire that had crashed.

Mr. Mason: Where did they come from - Rabaul?

Admiral Johnson: Rabaul.

Mr. Mason: Were there any Jap warships?

Admiral Johnson: None at all in the area.

The famous Tip Merrill was operating out there. He was in command of that cruiser division, and he'd had a very successful night action shortly before that.

Mr. Mason: Of which Arleigh Burke was a part.

Admiral Johnson: That's when Arleigh Burke's name first reached the headlines - thirty-one knot Burke. I suppose you know what started that - thirty-one knot Burke.

It was in one of those night engagements up there -- he had been alerted that there was a Japanese force coming down which was sent to meet them, and told to intercept them. He kept sending messages back down to Moumea at the headquarters, "Burke making thirty-one knots to intercept the enemy, Burke making thirty-one knots to intercept the enemy."

Ray Thurber, who was the operations officer down there,

finally sent one back, said, "Thirty-one knot Burke, you've got to get up off of your rear and make thirty-three if you're going to catch those boys." And he did.

That's why he was designated "thirty-one knot Burke." He was a great sailor.

Mr. Mason: You started to tell me why there weren't any Jap naval ships around.

Admiral Johnson: I think that they had been pretty badly knocked out by Tip Merrill with his cruiser division a few nights before that. Tip Merrill was one of the great men of the war - everybody was devoted to him, he was an inspirational leader.

We had no ships bother us. We landed our people on the beach, got our boats back, and just about sunset we sailed.

Mr. Mason: That was your mission - to land the troops and to leave and go back to Noumea?

Admiral Johnson: To get out of there and go to Guadalcanal first. Then, I think we went to Espirito Santos - maybe just to Guadalcanal. Because we loaded again as soon as we got there, and went back again. One week later we made our second landing on the beach.

Mr. Mason: With another contingent of Marines?

Admiral Johnson: Yes, another contingent of Marines.

My recollection is that at this time we had more difficulty from the air than we did the first time. It was possibly this time that I saw eight burning at one time, and a couple of Japanese planes come in. However, I did not lose any men the second time.

Mr. Mason: The beach head had been established.

Admiral Johnson: Yes.

A sad and tragic thing about the first one - I had thirty-one dead on board, somewhere around that; I'm not sure that we'd gotten all the bodies back. But we sailed and it was going to take us two and a half days to get back to Guadalcanal. It has a very depressing effect on men having dead people lying around, and also I was afraid they might begin to decompose. This was the first time this had ever happened to me, so I decided I'd bury them at sea.

Mr. Mason: That was your perogative, wasn't it?

Admiral Johnson: I thought it was, but it didn't turn out to be. I had them all laid out back on the fantail with weights attached to take them down. The Chaplain was all poised. I hoisted a general signal, which says that I'm preparing to bury the dead. I immediately got a signal back, "Negative, cancel."

Mr. Mason: From whom?

Admiral Johnson: From my division commander, a senior captain. He said they would be taken back to Guadalcanal. He told me later that their families had a right to have their bodies at home if they could get them to them.

What we did with them then -- the President Adams, having been around the world, had huge cold storage spaces in it. I should have thought of this before - we put them in there until we got back to Guadalcanal. They were taken ashore and buried there, but the families could get the body later if they wanted to. This was the only time I had that experience.

A week later we made the run in, and did not have any difficulty on the beach, but we did have a number of air attacks.

Mr. Mason: The same kind of time schedule - an early morning landing?

Admiral Johnson: Early morning landing the same time again.

Mr. Mason: Did the volcano cooperate again?

Admiral Johnson: I don't remember it the second time, maybe it had slowed down.

On the way back down the second time we were ordered to New Zealand. I think it was for rest and recreation for the crew, and to bring some more New Zealanders up. But when we got to Noumea we anchored there for overnight before sailing the next morning.

Early the next morning I heard four bongs - meaning a four-striper is coming aboard. So I went back to the gangway to meet him, a Captain I'd never seen before walked over the side and saluted and said, "Good morning, Captain, I'm your relief." "Why?" He said, "To relieve you. You've got to get your things in a hurry and get off, because we sail in an hour."

So I said, "Where am I going?" He said, "Here are your orders," and he gave me my orders. They were to the staff of the Commander-in-Chief of the South Pacific, Admiral Halsey's staff, but it didn't say what for.

Mr. Mason: But you knew you weren't in the dog house.

Admiral Johnson: I didn't think I was, no.

I rushed around and flung things in the bags and got off. I'd done a very dumb thing, which showed how little I knew about war -- I knew I might be around New Zealand and Australia a lot so I'd taken my golf clubs out when I first went out there. I forgot to take them ashore; I guess they stayed right with the President Adams, wherever it is. But I got everything else off and went ashore.

Mr. Mason: Tell me, sir - such a precipitious change in command for a ship like the President Adams - doesn't this put an unconscionable burden on the new officer?

Admiral Johnson: It's pretty hard on him unless you've got a good organization. Of course, the executive officer really runs the ship for the first few days after that. We did assemble the crew and I bade them good-bye and read my orders and went over the side. I had an excellent exec - this broker from New York - Charlie Spiegel. He could carry the weight of things. It is sort of rough on the Captain - not having any more time than that.

Mr. Mason: Not even knowing his way around the ship.

Admiral Johnson: No.
So I went ashore and went up and reported to the Commander-in-Chief South Pacific; actually I reported to the Chief of Staff, who was Admiral Robert B. Carney, in Noumea. I had known Admiral Carney slightly before . . .

Mr. Mason: You told me about that happenstance at the Naval Academy, when you sent him . . .

Admiral Johnson: This is the time it paid off; that's what caused me to be ordered to the staff. Admiral Carney and Admiral Halsey had decided that they needed a liaison officer to keep them in touch with General MacArthur. He would alternate back and forth between General MacArthur's headquarters and their headquarters. They hadn't had anybody before.

Mr. Mason: Where was MacArthur, Hollandia?

Admiral Johnson: MacArthur was alternating between Brisbane and Port Moresby in New Guinea. He hadn't gone to Hollandia yet - I went with him.

Admiral Carney explained all this to me. He said he thought the first thing for me to do would be to visit every post we had in the South Pacific, familiarize myself, and talk to the commanding officers there - find out what was available, what the facilities were, see what they could accommodate, and become well up on the South Pacific before I went to the other side.

Mr. Mason: That was a rather difficult thing to do, was it not? It was so fluid - the situation was changing . . .

Admiral Johnson: Yes. The fascination of it is that you have to be adaptable, you have to swing with the wind.

I spent the next three weeks flying all over the South Pacific.

Mr. Mason: Did you have a plane assigned for this purpose?

Admiral Johnson: No, I'd have to catch a ride. I'd stand with my thumb out and catch a ride.

Mr. Mason: How successful were you in thumbing a ride?

Admiral Johnson: Fine, except the first leg almost finished me. That was a PBM seaplane that was going from Noumea to Guadalcanal, and I got a ride. I was sitting there talking to a young man whom I'd never met before, John Endicott Lawrence from Boston, from Harvard, (He's the President of the John D. Lawrence Company.) He was the Air Combat Intelligence Officer of the South Pacific at that time. We were about two hundred miles out of Noumea when I had settled down and dropped back on a bunk to take a little nap, and I heard a commotion. I raised up and looked out the window; the port engine was one mass of flames. The pilot called back that he was putting it down, and get all the weight overboard. So we were throwing baggage out; I remember I heaved the machine gun out the port.

Mr. Mason: What was your altitude?

Admiral Johnson: We were going down very fast, going downwind; he couldn't turn around. I suppose we were about ten thousand feet when we started. But he did a splendid job - it was daylight in the morning. We dumped most things overboard, I lost all my luggage.

I remember one lad on board - he had been sent by his squadron in Guadalcanal down to New Zealand to get some whiskey for the mess. He had a tremendous bag full of whiskey, and as we were throwing things overboard I heard him say, "Oh, God, not that," and just then we hit the water. It was the next thing to go out the port, but we hit the water, so it wasn't necessary to throw it overboard. So he saved his precious cargo.

The pilot handled it extremely well. I think we floated for nine hours out there before somebody came to get us.

Mr. Mason: Were you able to put out the fire?

Admiral Johnson: Yes, we were able to put out the fire when we got to the water, when we got out on the wing. But we couldn't take off again. About nine hours later a PT-boat came out and got us.

Mr. Mason: You were able to communicate?

Admiral Johnson: On the way down they got a message off. I think they were not able to communicate after they got on the water.

They took us back to Noumea. The passengers were taken back in one PT-boat, and another PT-boat towed the plane and crew back.

Johnson #3 - 154

Mr. Mason: Were you in danger in that area of being straffed by Japs?

Admiral Johnson: No, there were none flying around there at all.

The next day we took off again, but this gave me an opportunity sitting around all this time to become friends with John E. Lawrence, which is one of the treasures of my life. He and his wife are among the most wonderful people that ever lived.

Mr. Mason: How many passengers were there stranded this way?

Admiral Johnson: About twenty or twenty-five.

Mr. Mason: What was your collective mood?

Admiral Johnson: Scared going down, and relieved after we got on the water, I think.

Mr. Mason: Was it rough?

Admiral Johnson: No, it wasn't very rough at all, not enough to make any of us seasick.

Mr. Mason: No great danger than that the PBM would sink?

Admiral Johnson: No, not at all. The difficult thing was landing it downwind; he couldn't turn around. He had to get it down as fast as he could.

Mr. Mason: What caused the engine to burst into flames?

Admiral Johnson: The pipe leading the gasoline into the carburator of the forward engine broke off under vibration and was just squirting raw gasoline on the cylinders. So we were lucky to get out of that.

I visited all the places in the South Pacific and got to know the commanding officers of them all.

Mr. Mason: Was that the only close call you had on your itinerary?

Admiral Johnson: No, I had a few others. On that itinerary that was the only one. It was fine with all the rest of them.

Mr. Mason: Where did you go?

Admiral Johnson: Just name every island down there; I went to them all. I even went back to Bougainville which was fairly well cleaned up by that time - it was three weeks after we went in. I went in there and spent four or five hours, talked to the Marines.

Mr. Mason: And really what was your aim, what were you trying . . .

Admiral Johnson: My aim was to know what was going on in the South Pacific so that when I got to the Southwest Pacific and I was asked over there -- what have you all got here, what's the mission of this place, what are you using this place for, that I could talk intelligently on them. I made notes which helped me.

Mr. Mason: Since it was such a fluid situation, did this mean that in this new assignment you had to repeat this operation again sometime soon in order to keep au courant?

Admiral Johnson: I think each time thereafter - I only went out once or twice more - when I got back to Noumea I would sit down with the operations officer and he would explain to me what changes had been made in the last two or three weeks since I was there.

On the 21st of December 1943 Admiral Carney had to go out to see General MacArthur, who was at Port Moresby. We flew out there from Noumea; I went with Admiral Carney. They had several members of the staff who wanted to go along to meet their opposite numbers on MacArthur's staff. And that's where I first met the General.

Actually my boss there, if I had one, was General Steve

Chamberlain - who died just last week - a wonderful man from Lynchburg, Virginia. He had a huge nose. He'd always say, "This is none of my business, but I'm going to stick my big proboscis in." I heard him say that so many times. He was the operations officer from MacArthur.

On the 24th Carney and everybody else left and went back to Noumea and left me out there. I felt isolated, pretty alone.

Mr. Mason: And your education was complete, you had acquired the background, now you're going to stay there.

Admiral Johnson: No, I stayed there half the time. But I had to stay there and familiarize myself with the way General MacArthur ran things, and his staff ran things.

So then from Port Moresby, after talking to the General a number of times, and his staff, I went to visit other posts that they had in Eastern New Guinea. They held Eastern New Guinea up not quite as far as Saidor at that time. I visited all the posts they had out there, and got to know the commanding officers.

And then General MacArthur went back to Brisbane, and I went back to Brisbane, too, and stayed about a week, and then back to Noumea and reported to Halsey what I thought was going on. From then on I alternated - one week on one side and one week on the other.

Mr. Mason: How close was the liaison between Halsey's staff and MacArthur's?

Admiral Johnson: I think it was pretty good, but I think it was naturally facilitated by the fact that I was there. I could go in and discuss any problem which we had in the South Pacific with the Southwest Pacific people, and vice versa. Because there was very little visiting back and forth, almost none. I only know of two times that people went over. But that was the idea of having me there.

Mr. Mason: This was before Kinkaid was there?

Admiral Johnson: Kinkaid was there at that time. I was also liaison officer to him, who I think was a splendid man, too. I enjoyed him very much. He had relieved Carpender; Carpender was there first.

Mr. Mason: Wasn't Fife also acting in some kind . . .

Admiral Johnson: He was in command of the submarines over in Western Australia at Perth.

Preparations were then underway for moving further up the coast of New Guinea, and I was allowed to sit in on all the planning for that in MacArthur's staff. Each time I'd go back to Noumea I would explain to our people what was going on and what was needed from them.

I guess it was in March - General MacArthur, as I remember it, told Admiral Kinkaid that he would like to have a naval aide for this landing at Hollandia. I don't know which one of them suggested me, whether it was Kinkaid or MacArthur, but I was designated as aide subject to Halsey's approval, which he immediately gave, of course.

Mr. Mason: What would your duties be as his aide for this particular operation?

Admiral Johnson: My job was to go along with him; we rode the Nashville in, and I was to be the liaison officer between the Army and the Navy -- between MacArthur's Army and Halsey and Nimitz's Navy.

I remember we sent a dispatch saying that there might be some Japanese air opposition from the fields in Western New Guinea, and asking Admiral Nimitz if he could supply - I think we asked for two carriers for air cover. God bless him, Admiral Nimitz, came back, "I will not supply two, I will send the entire force of carriers." I think it was something like fourteen or fifteen. So we had the most magnificent air cover you ever saw.

Of course, this just wrapped General MacArthur up. He usually didn't like Admiral Nimitz I think; there was a difference of opinions as to which way approach to Japan should be made; I guess an honest difference of opinions. General MacArthur wanted to go the southern route, and Admiral Nimitz wanted to go straight across. Sometimes when General MacArthur was rather annoyed about this he would refer to him as "Nimitz" but when he liked him he called him Admiral Nimitz. And he was really "Nimitz" all over the place after he put all these carriers there.

Mr. Mason: Had they not had a meeting in Australia prior to this?

Admiral Johnson: No, that happened later. I'm almost sure it was later, because I was in the receiving line making introductions at that time when Admiral Nimitz came down. He sent a dispatch down and said he would like to come down and call on him. Possibly it was before this, I'm not sure. It was to Brisbane.

Mr. Mason: Who accompanied Nimitz?

Admiral Johnson: I don't remember now, his aide (Hal Lamar).

I went out with the General to New Guinea. We spent about three nights in Port Moresby and then went over to the north side of the island. I think it was at Finschhafen that we boarded the Nashville, which had been assigned by Admiral Kinkaid to be the General's flag ship. The formation made up on that north shore. We went over to Manus Island first which had been taken a short while before that. Then from Manus we sailed for Hollandia.

The Pacific Fleet had given wonderful air cover and had beaten up the fields very badly, so we had no air opposition going in. There was opposition on the beaches. We made three simultaneous landings that day - Hollandia, Saidor, which was back towards Moresby, and there was one further up - Finschafen. We went ashore all three places that day.

General MacArthur was very much a combat guy. He went ashore I would say about an hour after the troops landed, at Hollandia. I went with him, and the Army aide.

A wonderful thing happened -- this Army aide I had known in Shanghai years before. He was the representative of Newsweek in Shanghai. I had known him out there. And it really saved my life, because when I got over to this assignment I found it very difficult to get in to see General MacArthur.

The Chief of Staff, General Sutherland, was, I think, a brilliant Chief of Staff, but he was always protective to the General - not only I, but a great many people found this to be true.

Mr. Mason: Was the General aware of this? Did he permit it willingly?

Admiral Johnson: I think he must have.

I know this time that I had the crisis there he kept me waiting twenty-four hours. I told him that I had an important message from Admiral Halsey for General MacArthur. He said, "I'll let you know when you can go in," and I waited twenty-four hours. He, I think, was just giving me a lesson.

When I finally did get in, I saw Larry Lehrbas - Colonel Larry Lehrbas was the Army aide. I was quite indignant by this time. I saw Larry there, who was my old friend of years before. And I told General MacArthur that I had been waiting twenty-four hours to deliver this message to him. He said, "In the future just tell Larry when you want to see me and you can see me any time you want to."

So as I went out I said to Sutherland, "General Sutherland, I will not bother you again when it's necessary for me to see General MacArthur. He has given me authority to come in and see him whenever I want to, so I won't bother you," and I never did again. Of course, he didn't like that, and I wouldn't have liked it if I'd been in his place either -- very presumptious of me.

Mr. Mason: But you had to meet the demands of your boss.

Admiral Johnson: I certainly did; I think he would have fired me if I hadn't been able to communicate his desires and requests.

Mr. Mason: That was the purpose of having you.

Admiral Johnson: Sure. But everything went fine; with Larry there I always got in, no trouble at all.

Larry and I accompanied General MacArthur ashore at Hollandia; we went in a PT-boat. On the way into the beach one hundred to one hundred and fifty yards off the beach, we had passed a tropical island very heavily covered with vegetation. This was about an hour after the troops had landed on the beach and had taken the beach, and weren't having very much difficulty really. When we landed we were standing on the beach talking to the general who commanded that area, when a machine gunner on this island we had passed opened up with a machine gun. It was his chance for fame forever if he'd killed General MacArthur. The bullets were zipping through trees up overhead. Larry and I were down digging for China. General MacArthur never hesitated in his talk to the general there. He never gave any indication at all that he'd heard this. I think he absolutely knew the bullet wasn't made that had his name. Someone on the beach opened up on the island and killed the Jap out there, but he missed killing General MacArthur by a very little bit.

Mr. Mason: MacArthur had this sense of destiny.

Admiral Johnson: I think he did absolutely, yes. I'm sure he did.

We stayed up on shore about an hour or so, and on the way back we were riding in a landing craft and we met the destroyer flying the flag of Admiral Fechteler, who commanded the naval forces at this landing. Admiral William Fechteler was an old friend of mine.

I told General MacArthur that this was Admiral Fechteler's flag ship. He thought that over a minute and said, "Can you wigwag?" He'd started calling me Felix by this time which pleased me; he said, "Felix, can you wigwag?"

Wigwag is pushing your flag to one side for a dot and the other side for a dash, and it went out in the Navy about 1915 or '16.

I said, "General, I can't wigwag, but I can semaphore." And he pointed at the engine frames and said, "Get up there and wigwag 'well done from MacArthur to Fechteler'." So I got up and went through that; that was my one signal I sent during that whole operation.

Mr. Mason: It was received?

Admiral Johnson: Received, yes, we got a receipt of thanks.

We went back aboard the Nashville and down to Saidor, which was twenty or thirty miles back down the beach. There we went ashore and looked over what was being accomplished.

Then we went back to the Nashville and went twenty or thirty miles on the other side of Hollandia to the third landing, and we went ashore there.

Then when we got back, as I remember it, we went down to

Finschhafen. I believe we disembarked at Finschhafen and flew back.

It was a great privilege to sit with the General; I messed with him at all the meals, with him and Larry. I got to know him well and felt that we were friends when this was over.

About that time it became apparent that the fighting was over in the South Pacific, so Admiral Carney wrote a letter to the Bureau of Personnel saying that I could be spared from down there. So I was ordered home in command of a cruiser.

Mr. Mason: May I ask you a question - about the Nashville, the President Adams, and all the other ships seemingly going with ease from one island to another, weren't there navigational problems? Were the charts adequate?

Admiral Johnson: I think we had pretty good charts that the Dutch had made out there. I wouldn't say that about the Yangtze; I used to run aground all the time with my gunboat up the Yangtze, the currents were changing all the time. But I don't remember any groundings out there, so they must have been good charts that we had.

Mr. Mason: And a grounding was your least concern anyway, wasn't it?

Admiral Johnson: Yes, we had some other concerns besides that.

Mr. Mason: Tell me about the role of the Army Air Force in the New Guinea operations.

Admiral Johnson: George Kenny was in command of the Army Air Force and I think they did a fine job. He was not very close to the Navy officials out there - General Kenny - nor they to him.

Mr. Mason: Was this his personality?

Admiral Johnson: I think it was. There had been a little friction between air forces I think for some time, even before the war. This had not been overcome at that time, but I think it has now. But we got along all right. General Kenny certainly put on some wonderful air cover that day out there, with our Navy planes, too.

Mr. Mason: There were problems, were there not, in going over the island itself - the Owen Stanley Range?

Admiral Johnson: Oh yes, the Owen Stanley Range - a very formidable thing. I flew over those many times.
    We had a little island called Goodenough, on the north shore

of New Guinea. It had an airfield on it; I landed there a number of times.

Vice Admiral Felix Johnson, USN, Ret.   Interview #4

U. S. Naval Institute

January 12, 1972

By: John T. Mason, Jr.

Mr. Mason: Admiral, it's great to see you again this morning. I've been looking forward to this interview.

Last time you concluded by talking about your assignment as special aide to General MacArthur, representing Halsey and the Navy, during the Hollandia landing. After that you were detached from your liaison job, but before we leave that would you give me as estimate of General MacArthur as a military figure and focus on him for a bit.

Admiral Johnson: Dr. Mason, I think I was highly privileged to be so associated with General MacArthur. It was a tremendous opportunity to observe a great man at work, and to observe him closely.

He had some weaknessess, I'm sure, as everybody has. I think he was possibly a little vain, and sometimes he might be a bit lacking in a sense of humor. But he had a tremendous talent for leadership; everyone that I knew that served with him was deeply devoted to him.

It was especially heartwarming and satisfying to see how well he and my real boss, Admiral Halsey got along. They admired each other a great deal.

Mr. Mason: They had something in common, didn't they?

Admiral Johnson: Yes, they did. They were unique, each one of them was. They were very different men. I think possibly one of their differences would be simplified by a little thing like the name tag that they wore on their field jackets. Admiral Halsey, Commander of the South Pacific, had on his "William F. Halsey, Admiral, United States Navy." General MacArthur had "MacArthur." That is sort of the difference - that distinguishes them.

Mr. Mason: But they both had a certain flamboyance.

Admiral Johnson: Oh, great flamboyance, very much of a flamboyance.

General MacArthur, as I witnessed him in action, was utterly fearless - he just knew the bullet wasn't made that had his name on it; nobody could ever knock him off. He had the greatest confidence in the future.

He had tremendous imagination. I don't think he tolerated opposition very well. He wanted his way when he wanted it, but he was right so damn often that I don't see how anybody could quarrel with that.

Of course there was throughout that part of the war and some time later a difference of opinion among the leaders as to which way to go to make the approaches to Japan. General

MacArthur was sure that it should be made by going back to the Philippines. And I think possibly this may have been contributing a little weakness there, because he had been so humiliated in having to evacuate the Philippines, and leave in a PT-boat, and leave his troops there - this very nearly killed him. He wanted to go back and wipe all that out. Whereas, Admiral King and the General Staff in Washington felt that the approach should be straight across the Pacific, the most direct route. And this sort of handed the ball to Nimitz instead of MacArthur. They went both ways, as you know, and I think that was probably the wisest thing to do.

Going back to the Hollandia operation a minute - I think it was a simply amazing thing that he did in making that jump - that run around the Japanese, some three hundred miles I believe it was - by-passing all the thousands and thousands and thousands of troops that were left to starve and die on the vine, on the North New Guinea coast, and to avoid fighting them to go make the landing in their rear. We landed at Aitape, Hollandia, and Tanahmerah Bay - simultaneous landings at those three - and just cut off probably a hundred thousand Japanese that were left down the coast line. And it was made almost without loss - the whole operation. It was applauded by Halsey; Halsey thought it was a wonderful thing that he did.

I never observed any friction between those two men at all; they gave each other complete support.

Mr. Mason: That was rather remarkable, because they were both . . .

Admiral Johnson: . . . such flamboyant characters, with their personalities it was amazing. A great deal of that I think was due to Admiral Carney.

Admiral Carney was a very brilliant, very sharp, very smooth, and personable man, and he had charge of the inter-relations with MacArthur. He made more trips to Australia than Admiral Halsey did; Admiral Halsey would come over occasionally. When I was first assigned to this task Admiral Carney - God bless him - flew me all the way up to New Guinea to be sure that I met General MacArthur, and had access to him, and that General MacArthur understood that I was speaking for Admiral Halsey when I came over there. He had a great deal to do with operations.

Mr. Mason: That was his way of working. He escorted you over there?

Admiral Johnson: He probably would have gone for some other reason about the same time. He made trips every once in awhile, but he insured that I went with him and met MacArthur through him. He was a very great naval officer.

I am just filled with admiration for General MacArthur. I had the great pleasure later, when I worked with Intelligence in Washington, going out to Japan when Korea broke, of meeting

General MacArthur again. We had a very heartwarming reunion; I had lunch with him in Tokyo.

Mr. Mason: Did you find him equally as brilliant then as he was earlier?

Admiral Johnson: Yes, I did. In my opinion his hands were tied; I deplored the fact that he wasn't allowed to go ahead and win that war. I deplored, if I may say so, the fact that he was relieved of his job as he was. I was in the Pentagon and went to the theater the day he was to make his farewell talk to Congress; the whole thing was so dismal that I just faded away. This theater was just packed with people, standing room only. When he finally gave those last words people were weeping all over the room - really an amazing thing.

He had a lovely wife whom I met a number of times. I had lunch with her in Tokyo the last time I was out there. She was a dedicated church woman; she went to church every Sunday, in Brisbane. I saw her there a time or two. She was a lovely person. She always referred to him as The General; I don't know if that's what she called him to his face or not.

Mr. Mason: How do you account then for the fact that MacArthur's relations with many of the other commanders was not the best? He got along with Halsey all right, but there were others with whom he did not. How do you account for the fact that here was a brilliant man aware of so much, and yet lacking in diplomatic finesse, shall we say?

Admiral Johnson: I think that a lot of it was envy of less successful men. That certainly is not true about Nimitz, but he really had good relations with Nimitz, but more due to Nimitz I think than to General MacArthur.

Possibly I've spoken of this before -- I always thought it was a wonderful thing for Admiral Nimitz to do to get in his plane and fly all the way down to Australia to call on General MacArthur to put his Air at MacArthur's disposal in this Hollandia operation.

Mr. Mason: There is so much evidence in the Nimitz material that the Admiral really didn't care for General MacArthur.

Admiral Johnson: There is? I didn't know that.

But he swallowed his pride -- he went down to confer with him and to give General MacArthur all the assistance that he possibly wanted. That was the only time that I had the opportunity to observe him with Admiral Nimitz.

Mr. Mason: But MacArthur didn't make any special effort or overtures toward people who didn't really admire him, did he?

Admiral Johnson: I can't think of anybody down there who really didn't like him, except some at the very junior level, and that's because they never knew him. His seclusion was his greatest weakness, in my opinion.

Mr. Mason: That was by choice, was it?

Admiral Johnson: I feel a great deal of it was because of his Chief of Staff. His Chief of Staff, I felt then and I still believe, wanted to seclude him in order to enhance his own power. Possibly I shouldn't say that about the man, but that's the way it seemed to me.

Mr. Mason: Why would the General, if he was not in agreement, permit this?

Admiral Johnson: I don't quite know.

Maybe I said this before -- Oh my last visit with General MacArthur I said, "General, may I make a suggestion before I leave?"

Mr. Mason: This was in the South Pacific?

Admiral Johnson: In the South Pacific; I was under orders home then.

He said, "Certainly, go ahead." He called me Felix then. I said, "You were a very remote person to me until I was assigned to this job. I read a lot about you, but didn't know you at all.

"I find that there are a great many people in your own forces over here who don't know you at all, who've never had any opportunities of seeing you. When the staff conferences are held here they are conducted by the Chief of Staff, not you. If you would simply walk in to the staff conference the last ten or fifteen minutes, if you couldn't devote more time to it, and ask a few questions, and let the officers there see you operate, I think it would change the picture a great deal."

He didn't resent at all my making the suggestions, but I don't know whether he ever did it or not.

I know that later my friend, Admiral Turner Joy, who was the naval commander in Japan and Korea, had very close relations with him and had access to him at all times, and admired him very much.

So for me it was a very great experience and a very great privilege to be associated with him.

Mr. Mason: Would you tell me a little about Manus - how it was selected as a base for repairing ships and what have you?

Admiral Johnson: At that time I'm afraid I wasn't in on that much.

It's position was most ideal. As I remember it, it was about two to five degrees south lattitude, and it was further advanced than Cape Gloucester which we had taken at that time. There was an excellent harbor there, and it just seemed to be absolutely ideal.

I believe - I'm not sure of this - that this was a combined operation of the Southwest Pacific and the Central Pacific - the taking of Manus. I think the Central Pacific supplied all the Air. As I remember it also, there wasn't a great deal of resistance, but it just made an ideal place.

I went in there three times I believe. With General MacArthur when we were in the Nashville on the way to Tanahmerah Bay we paused briefly in Manus. As a matter of fact we refueled there, and went on.

It was a staging area for the further advance, and it was an ideal one.

Mr. Mason: But it was made into a considerable base for repairing ships.

Admiral Johnson: Yes, ships that had gotten beaten up would come back here to be repaired. Otherwise, they would have had to go all the way back to Pearl Harbor.

Mr. Mason: Whose vision was that?

Admiral Johnson: I think that probably was Nimitz; I don't think this was General MacArthur.

Johnson #4 - 177

Mr. Mason: You were cited as being instrumental in some of this . . .

Admiral Johnson: Yes, I have noticed that, but I'm afraid I can't claim that credit. It was probably just wanting to put something in my award there. But really my operations were in the Southwest Pacific; I was only there three times, and not very actively.

I did, a number of times, take messages back and forth to the Southwest Pacific and vice versa, as to how we were going about taking Manus, but I was not in the operation actually.

Mr. Mason: But when the base was established you went there -- what purpose did you have then?

Admiral Johnson: I went there with General MacArthur once, and I flew in once going to Hollandia, and once coming back from Hollandia, but only briefly over a day. This award is really not merited.

You certainly would be justified in asking me those questions, but I didn't do much planning for that.

I did have something to do with the transfer of troops back and forth from the Southwest Pacific to the South Pacific. Most everything was going from the South Pacific to the Southwest Pacific because we had just taken over our area - only Rabaul was left.

Mr. Mason: What did you do in the transfer of troops?

Admiral Johnson: We would establish a date in which the command of a unit would pass from the South Pacific to the Southwest Pacific, and General MacArthur would then decide where they were to go in the Southwest Pacific.

Mr. Mason: They were entering his command?

Admiral Johnson: They were coming under his command.

We would make strikes for the Southwest Pacific and they would make strikes for us. They helped cover the Bougainville operation. I think they undertook the neutralization of Rabaul, which was very heavily fortified. I'm awfully glad we never tried to take Rabaul, that would have been a murderous operation.

Mr. Mason: After your mission with General MacArthur was completed, what did you do then?

Admiral Johnson: Then I received orders to return to the United States and to command a light cruiser called the Springfield, which was under construction at the Fall River Yard outside of Boston.

So I came home, flew home of course, and had a couple weeks leave with my family in Annapolis where they were.

Then I went up to Boston. My ship was within about two months of being completed.

Mr. Mason: This was a speed-up job, was it?

Admiral Johnson: Yes, very much of a speed-up job.

It was a wonderful opportunity again. I think there was an omen of good fortune in it, because my roommate at the Naval Academy was from Springfield, Massachusetts - a wonderful man. I spent the night with him last night. (He now lives in Pendennis Mount.)

So I loved having that name, and I always liked the city of Springfield. And the Navy Department gave me a wonderful group of officers and crew.

Mr. Mason: What sort of complement did the Springfield have?

Admiral Johnson: I think it was about fourteen hundred, with about seventy-five to ninety officers.

Mr. Mason: Were they all on deck when you arrived there?

Admiral Johnson: No, they streamed in over the next two months. I'd say about a fourth of them were there.

Mr. Mason: What did you do in that interim period before . . .

Admiral Johnson: We tried to get the ship organized, and to learn our way around, and to plan our future operations. I did some negotiating with the Bureau of Personnel about some of the officers to come. I flew down to Washington. They were most cooperative in sending ones I wanted.

Mr. Mason: It was people you knew?

Admiral Johnson: A few of them were, yes. I would look up the talents of the person. I felt they were letting me down in the case of one - the supply officer. They had a junior lieutenant assigned, and I rather wanted to get my supply officer from the President Adams to come there. But the Bureau of Personnel said no.

I found out that actually this was in error; this was a lieutenant commander instead of a junior lieutenant. He turned out to be the ablest supply officer that I'd ever known, and he's served me in several other capacities since then. He's a retired Captain in the Judge Advocate General's Corps - Captain Herbert Schwab.

Mr. Mason: So your judgment wasn't . . .

Admiral Johnson: No, it was completely wrong.

I had a wonderful executive officer, Commander E. P. Southwick, an aviator, and a marvelous chaplain, a Catholic chaplain,

Father Lane. He was just as dedicated to looking after the welfare of the Protestants or the people who had no religion as he was the Catholics on board.

Mr. Mason: That's the tradition of the Navy Chaplains, sir.

Admiral Johnson: It certainly was, and he was one of the best.

Mr. Mason: I suppose the Springfield was being outfitted with a lot of new equipment.

Admiral Johnson: Yes, we were, we were getting a lot of which to me, of course, was new. I had an extremely able gunnery officer who had come from being assistant gunnery officer of the Columbia so had been familiar with all of this stuff.

If I may tell you one little thing about gunnery -- the day the ship was commissioned it was towed over to the Boston Yard to be commissioned. My dear old friend, Commodore Charles Francis Adams, came down for the commissioning. He stepped out of his car at the foot of the gangway, he started up the gangway and looked down at the ground and stopped to pick up something. He brought it up and handed it to me - it was a penny that he had found. He said if I would put this under the foot of my foremast the Springfield would always have good luck. So we welded that to the foremast.

We had two sponsors, I don't remember their names now.

The ship was named for Springfield, Massachusetts and Springfield, Illinois. They chose different sponsors, as you can imagine. The one from Springfield, Illinois was a charming beautiful young lady, a high school senior I suppose - she was lovely. Springfield, Massachusetts chose an old Italian lady who had five children in the Navy - four sons and a daughter. She was about seventy years old, I suppose, and she was simply marvelous. She gave us a St. Christopher medal for the commissioning of the Springfield. We welded that to the forward edge of the bridge, so that I could touch it for luck any time we had a tough operation coming up.

I remember I had a first class petty officer named Negro, who was a delightful man, but he was a good Catholic. He was rather critical I think of my depending on luck in touching this thing when I had a hard landing or something like that to make.

Later off Okinawa, kamikazes were running fast and furious, and one made a run on us one day. He came down in a vertical dive. Negro was the JA talker; he stood right back of me on the bridge to pass orders throughout the ship. This thing was coming down in a straight dive. We were making thirty-five knots; I had hard right rudder on and dodging and he just missed. I think the edge of his plane hit the after catapult when he went into the water. But we were going so fast that by the time his bomb exploded we had passed a hundred yards or something like that from him; it didn't hurt us at all. But when he went out of sight behind the mast I thought he had us in the stern, and everybody else did. There was a big sigh of relief from everybody, and a hand came over my shoulder – it was Negro – touching the St. Christopher medal. He said, "Captain, I think I'll take a piece of that, too."

Mr. Mason: Was the Springfield equipped with radar?

Admiral Johnson: Oh yes.

Mr. Mason: Did this require any special training prior to her commissioning?

Admiral Johnson: Yes, all of our radar men had been to school and trained in this particular equipment.

The Navy had some most excellent schools. They had fire control, they had studied all about fire control.

We had one gunner's mate – this is a small thing – who made a suggestion. As far as I know it was the first time it had ever been done, and I think it was very effective.

All the guns on the ship were six-inch guns in the turrets, and five-inch anti-aircraft guns -- they were on all the levels.

The day we were commissioned there was a great crowd of distinguished people, and families, and friends down to watch it, of course. All the guns were laid on the level and he suggested that we tie all the guns electrically to one director so that when you moved the director it would move all the guns in the ship at the same time. So as the ship was placed in commission the Star Spangled Banner played and the flag hoisted slowly, he cranked the director and all the guns went up together following the flag - they were all pointing to the flag. You could just hear a sigh from the whole group.

Mr. Mason: That was truly dramatic.

Admiral Johnson: Terribly dramatic. I think it was generally adopted after that, but this was a fire controlman who thought that up.

Mr. Mason: But they were capable of operating separately?

Admiral Johnson: Oh yes, of course. That was just for that one time.

The Governor of Massachusetts was there for the commissioning, and Admiral Theobald who commanded the naval district at that time, and my dear friend Mr. Adams was there. When we sailed on our shakedown cruise Mr. Adams went with me as far as Norfolk. There was a lot of firing on the way down, and he wanted to see that. We flew him back up. He was the ex-Secretary of the Navy.

Mr. Mason: What did you do to prepare yourself for some of

this new equipment, like radar. How much knowledge did you have to have?

Admiral Johnson: I had, of course, been through the ship many many times, inspecting everything on it and having things explained to me. I didn't and don't pretend to understand the operation of all this complicated gear, except in the most general way. This was for the gunnery officer and the electricians and the fire controlmen to do, but they were constantly briefing me on what they were doing.

I don't think I went to school anywhere, but I did go aboard every ship of the same class built at roughly the same time that I could and had talks with the captain of those ships, as to what their problems were and what they had done to surmount them.

I had a first class master-at-arms on board who was in civilian life; a motorcycle policeman from Pennsylvania. We were trying to make the ship very smart.

So when the inspecting officer went through a compartment, as he entered the compartment the man in charge of the compartment would salute him and say, "Good morning, Captain, good morning Admiral. This is compartment C402 storage room," or whatever it was. This man had been briefed in that.

Finally the man who was going to be my Admiral in the Pacific came up to Boston to inspect my ship - this was just before we sailed on the shakedown cruise - Admiral Cary Jones.

As he entered the crew's messing compartment, of which he was in charge -- and by the way, they were all to give their names and rates. You would say, "This is the crew's messing compartment, John Mason boatswain first class in charge." We entered his compartment - he was a very fine looking tall handsome man named John Papadopoulous. He drew himself up and said, "Good morning Admiral, crew's messing compartment C103, John John son-of-a-bitch Admiral, I can't say it." I think the Admiral had the grace to smile instead of being irritated by that.

We commissioned her in Boston and. . .

Mr. Mason: You knew where you were destined to go?

Admiral Johnson: Yes, we knew where we were destined to go.

About a month later we sailed on our shakedown cruise, down as far as Norfolk, doing some firing on the way down, aerial towed target was given us on the way down, went into the Bay and did some shooting at surface targets in the Bay . . .

Mr. Mason: Did you have escort on the way down?

Admiral Johnson: I don't remember, I think we probably did. There was a lot of submarine activity. I know a little later we didn't have one; I'll speak of that in a moment.

Then we completed our firing in the Bay. This involved training and refueling at sea on the way down. We had some experience in the operation.

Mr. Mason: But that was not a new technique for you?

Admiral Johnson: I had done it a few times in a destroyer; I'd never done it in a ship as big as this - it was the same problem really.

Mr. Mason: What was her tonnage?

Admiral Johnson: I think it was about twenty thousand tons.

I had been alerted - this last trip I had made to Washington I had been asked to come to the Chief of Naval Operations and was told that we were going to accompany the President on part of his voyage to Yalta. He was sailing from Norfolk in the Iowa for Yalta. This was January 1945.

We went into Hampton Roads and anchored there for a couple of days until the President was ready to leave. Then we sailed with the Iowa, there were also three or four destroyers. I was the only large ship in the escort.

We accompanied him as far as the Azores, and there we were met by another cruiser that relieved me. I was detached and ordered to Pearl Harbor. Then we did sail from the Azores to Panama with no escort, across a large stretch of ocean, and transited the Canal.

There, of course, was great secrecy about this voyage of

the President. There was a question when we left as to whether I could bid him adieu or not. As we left, we didn't say anything about the President - we finally resolved that by sending a message to the Captain of the Iowa asking him to deliver our respects and admiration to their distinguished passenger and signed it from the officers and crew of the Springfield.

We transited the Canal, and again without escort we had a long run across the ocean direct from Panama to Pearl.

Mr. Mason: What speed would you achieve?

Admiral Johnson: As I remember it we could only do sixteen and still have enough fuel to get there; we had to be careful about that. And I'm not quite sure that I zigzagged all the time, which I should have but I was trying to save fuel to be sure that we got in. You remember the Indianapolis was later torpedoed when she was not zigzagging and this might have happened to me. A classmate of mine Charlie McVay was the Captain of the Indianapolis, and that might have happened to me. But we got to Pearl . . .

As I remember it we only had about a week there before we sailed for the Okinawa operation. During this week we, of course, refueled, refitted a few things that didn't work, and had a few additions to the crew there, and then sailed . . .

Mr. Mason: May I ask you - what about your fire control on board; how thorough was that?

Admiral Johnson: That was excellent, splendid. Captain Robert Sleight was the gunnery officer . . .

Mr. Mason: I meant damage control.

Admiral Johnson: I think that was very adequate indeed. We had all been through damage control schools, including myself. I had a splendid damage control officer, and fortunately we were never tested by being hit.

Mr. Mason: I suppose the most recent experiences in the Pacific were all available?

Admiral Johnson: All available to us. The damage control people from the Commander-in-Chief's staff were aboard our ship checking on everything we were doing and giving us the benefit of the practical experience which they had had out in the war that we were all green to. Most of us had been in some part of the war in other ships, but there were a lot of green hands on board, too.

Mr. Mason: What was the morale like on board in your crew?

Admiral Johnson: I'm a biased person, of course, but I think it was splendid. They all were proud of being in a new ship, and they were all proud of what they were doing to it.

I can remember, if I may again give an instance, the day the ship was commissioned in Boston. The prospective commanding officer normally makes a talk to the crew. I listed in my little talk some of the great ships from which they had come - some were from the Lexington, some from the Iowa, some from the South Dakota, people who had been through the war already. I pointed out how terribly fortunate we were to have men of that caliber and that experience to whom war was nothing new, and they could impart that knowledge to us who hadn't seen so much of the war, and it was in their hands whether this ship was going to be another South Dakota or whether it was going to be . . .

Mr. Mason: Making a challenge to them collectively.

Admiral Johnson: Yes, and they certainly responded magnificently.

Mr. Mason: That was a neat way of handling people who had been on ships that had sunk and who had that traumatic experience in their background.

Admiral Johnson: I hope it was, it seemed to be well received.

Mr. Mason: Did the Commander-in-Chief come aboard?

Admiral Johnson: No, I called on him, of course. There were just too many ships going in and out that he couldn't get to all of them.

The Admiral with whom I was going to work was in there at the same time in the Pasadena, and he came aboard - Cary Jones.

I don't believe we sailed with the Pasadena. We had a couple of destroyers with us. We sailed from there for Ulithi, and at Ulithi the big fleet was forming up for the Okinawa operation. I think we were only there three days before we sailed for Okinawa.

Mr. Mason: What was your specific position to be?

Admiral Johnson: I was to be part of the Task Force which was operating there, Task Force 58. There were four groups in that - Task Force 58 - 1, 2, 3, and 4. As I remember it I was part of Task Force 3, and the Admiral of which was Sherman (not Forrest Sherman; the other Sherman). A very able and splendid officer he was, too.

I was in the screen that surround the carriers; we had, I believe three carriers in our group. There was first the cruisers and battleships screen, and then further out a destroyer screen. We operated there as a group turning and weaving together, all signals were given by TBS. They had to be understood and action taken quite promptly when kamikazes were running around. The Task Force was operating at very high speed, thirty to thirty-five knots, and turning and weaving to avoid the kamikazes, and to keep the carriers into the wind at the right time, and then going back downwind when the planes were not landing and taking off in order to keep station more or less - a very complicated operation.

Mr. Mason: The kamikaze attack, as it developed, was this anticipated?

Admiral Johnson: I don't think it was anticipated anything like the extent to which we had. We'd had a few before. One kamikaze came in to Hollandia - that was a very early one. As I remember it, this was after we had taken the harbor and had established a base ashore. He saw the lights on the wharf and thought it was a ship and plunged into the water instead of the ship. We had some kamikazes, but nothing like we were to get later on. The whole Japanese effort almost was kamikazes later.

Mr. Mason: What was the reaction to this one down in Hollandia - one of the first ones? What did you think about this technique? Did you recognize it as a technique?

Admiral Johnson: I thought it was very unfair, that's what the Americans would think. We didn't realize that it was going to be such a horrible thing as it became later.

Mr. Mason: You thought it was unfair for the aviator, to assign him to such a mission as that?

Admiral Johnson: Yes, but I found out later that they were all volunteers for it.

I think one of the greatest things about the Okinawa operation to me was how long ships could stay at sea, how long we could stay out there. We would drop back about one hundred miles further away from Japan every fourth night, and the next morning we would fall in with tankers, hospital ships, supply ships, and we would be assigned in rotation to go alongside. We'd go alongside and secure, we'd send over by line anybody who was due to go home, bring back new men that the tankers had brought out for us. If we had any people very seriously ill or injured on board they would go alongside the hospital ship and send them over on a stretcher. I was on the line somewhere between ninety and one hundred days, and at the end of that time we had just as much fuel, just as much ammunition, - we went to an ammunition ship for replenishment, too - and just as many men as we had when we came out there, due to this wonderful operation that they'd developed of the Service Fleet. It was simply splendid.

Mr. Mason: Would you be willing to speculate on the possibility of the Okinawa victory if we had not had the Service Fleet developed, if ships had had to fall back to a supply base.

Admiral Johnson: I should think it would have taken six months to a year longer, and we'd have lost a great many more ships and men than we did if we hadn't had this operation. It was just wonderful. Admiral Donald B. Beary was in command of this; he had been my Captain in the destroyer many years before. He was one of the best ship handlers I've ever seen, and one of the ablest officers I've ever known.

Mr. Mason: Looking at it from a different point of view — the development of this Service Fleet made it possible to stay on station great lengths of time, but what did this do to the personnel being constantly subjected to battle conditions, say for ninety days as you were?

Admiral Johnson: I'm sure it was rough on us all, but I think they and I were proud of what we were being able to accomplish, and they knew that they weren't there indefinitely. Some of them went off every fourth day; this was a planned operation that some sailors went off and some came on every fourth day. And though it might be just a symbolic replenishment of men, they could leave and they could come aboard and they all realized that.

Mr. Mason: So it wasn't beyond human endurance. Were there any crackups on your ship?

Admiral Johnson: Yes, I had a very distressing one. I had a young ensign on board who cracked up and was put in sick bay until he could be transferred the next day to the hospital ship. We were going to refuel and replenish the next day and go alongside, and in the middle of the night he disappeared from the ship. He somehow got out of sick bay without anyone seeing him, which was bad. But he did get out, got up on deck, jumped overboard, and after hitting the water he decided he'd made a mistake, so he went to swimming. This sounds incredible, but eight hours later the Task Force went through the same water that we had been in when he jumped overboard and a destroyer saw him and picked him up and transferred him to the hospital ship. He was sent back to America and recovered and went back on duty again. That was extraordinary - eight hours he was in the water.

The people that had the roughest time, of course, were the destroyers that were stationed out on the picket line - twenty-five to fifty miles ahead of us, because they were the first ones the kamikazes were most likely to attack because they did not know what they were attacking. Quite a number of them were in very perilous state. They came back every fourth day also; they'd come in to the Force to refuel from one of us before they went back out on the line again.

I remember this destroyer - his code name was Boar Tusk. The Captain had a very well developed sense of humor because he came back dashing through the picket line, going right through the formation to turn around and come back to fuel, and he had a sheet handing over the side and written on it in big letters, "Jap aviator, don't stop here. Task Force 58 twenty-five miles in this direction," with an arrow pointing toward the stern. This was a naval officers named George Demotropolius; I always enjoyed him being around. That was greatly applauded when he went through the screen.

Mr. Mason: I would think a sense a humor under those circumstances was a rather essential thing.

Admiral Johnson: It was indeed, it was wonderful.

Mr. Mason: Did you maintain yours?

Admiral Johnson: I tried to, but I think I got awfully serious some times. Some of my officers would keep me from getting too serious, I think. I had a wonderful group; many of them did have great senses of humor. The Chaplain was one of the best of all.

I went through this about ninety days . . .

Mr. Mason: Did you have any other close calls in addition to the one you described a little earlier?

Admiral Johnson: We had some quite near misses.

Mr. Mason: You were the prospective target for other kamikazes?

Admiral Johnson: Yes, but they were usually trying for the carriers. They might hit near me, but they probably would have passed over me heading for the carriers. We were only about five to eight hundred yards from the carriers.

Mr. Mason: You were a secondary target for those.

Admiral Johnson: Yes, I think a secondary target.

I was very near the Franklin when she was hit, and there was another one. I've forgotten the name of the carrier; it was my friend Bob Hickey's carrier. I was within five hundred yards of it when a kamikaze in a vertical dive took them just aft of the conning tower - the island - of this carrier.

Quite often many men would go over the side when these ships would be hit. They'd be blown over the side, or they had to jump over the side to escape the fire. The destroyers would try to pick them up. The big ships - we weren't allowed to pick them up; we had to keep going. It was horrible to see a bunch of men in the water and you had to try to avoid them and go through them at high speed, and not try to rescue them.

Mr. Mason: But there were regular rescue ships.

Admiral Johnson: Yes, assigned for that task. They did a

splendid job, too.

Mr. Mason: The men knew this?

Admiral Johnson: Oh yes.

The only wounded I had were due to target difficulty. When a kamikaze is making a vertical or nearly vertical dive and some fifteen or twenty ships are shooting at him as he comes down, there's a great danger that you're going to follow it too long and still be shooting when he gets down along the water and the ships are in your line - that required very high discipline. I'm afraid that one of my guns hit the <u>Missouri</u>; it could have been my ship or it could have been several others. I remember that we had followed that one down too far, and it hit their conning tower. I had a few people wounded by fragments from ships; people that were following it down - one that was making a run for us. We were just terribly blessed that we didn't have anybody die to the best of my recollection while we were there. Anyone who was seriously ill, of course, was transferred to the hospital ship.

And then, one morning a yeoman came in, followed by the executive officer, and said, "We've got a message for you." It was detaching me and ordering me back to the Bureau of Personnel as Director of Plans and Policy. It became later Pers-A.

Mr. Mason: This was after a ninety day stint there.

Admiral Johnson: Yes, ninety days on the line. I'd only been in the ship about a year.

Mrs. Mason: Why the rapid transfer?

Admiral Johnson: I really can't say, except that I had known several of the senior officers who were in BuPers at that time, and the man who was filling that billet, Captain Hillenkoetter, later Admiral, had been there for something over two years and he wanted to go to sea, so they ordered me there.

Mr. Mason: The battle was over, however?

Admiral Johnson: No.

Mr. Mason: It was difficult to be extricated at that point, wasn't it?

Admiral Johnson: It was indeed, it was quite upsetting.

Mr. Mason: How did your men feel about it?

Admiral Johnson: I think they'd learned to get along very well together by that time. I hope some of them regretted it; I certainly did.

Captain Thomas J. Kelly was ordered as my relief. The next run down to the replenishing unit he came aboard by the high line from one of the tankers there.

Mr. Mason: And you went by the same route?

Admiral Johnson: I did, three days later. He stayed with me during those three days. They were pretty brisk days, so he got a very good breaking in.

Mr. Mason: How do you make your way back to the States under those circumstances?

Admiral Johnson: I was transferred to a destroyer by the high line again.

Kelly relieved me on the morning of the fourth day, and I bid farewell to everybody, got in the high line seat and was taken over to a destroyer which went alongside a light, what they called, jeep carrier, the Bougainville. It's mission was to take off planes from the carriers which had been damaged, and had to be carried back to shore to have major overhaul. They took on, I suppose, thirty or forty planes. Then we sailed for Guam.

The Captain was named Bevo Bond - I haven't seen him for a long time. But just last week I saw the executive officer, who was Admiral Thomas South -- a perfectly wonderful man who has had physical handicaps since he had a heart attack.

I remember an amusing thing about that -- we were entering Guam. We had been at sea probably two or three weeks and we were glad to get in behind the nets, and not to have to dread the kamikazes and submarines anymore. As we stood up to the entrance, there was a blinking light from the signal tower, a message said, "Bougainville, keep clear of the harbor. Commander Third Fleet (Halsey) is in your berth. Wait until he moves."

Bond was very annoyed, of course. So we had to turn around and go back out. He said to Tommy South, "Tell Halsey to get the hell out of my berth." We went out and steamed around, and in about twenty minutes Tommy South said, "Your message sent and receipted." He said, "What message do you mean?" He had it all written up, "Bougainville to the Commander Third Fleet - get the hell out of my berth." Captain Bond almost fainted.

This was just a frame-up on the Captain -- it's lighthearted things like that which relieve the monotony of seagoing.

Mr. Mason: Tell me - just the psychological factor intrigues me -- you are a man under authority, you are in a berth, and you're Captain of the Springfield, and you're engaged in battle and don't want to leave; and all of a sudden you're commanded to leave and go back to Washington.

Admiral Johnson: I think you learn to carry out your orders always. It is in a way flattering to be chosen for a job like that. I doubt very much if I'd ever been a flag officer if I hadn't gone to that job. It makes you well known, and gives you the opportunity to serve.

So from Guam I flew to Pearl, and got another plane and flew back to Washington, changing again in San Francisco. I had, I think, three weeks leave before taking over this new job.

It was not as exciting, of course, as the Springfield, but again a very rewarding job. The war was fast winding to a close, and you should be able to see so many problems which were going to arise at this time - instead of hauling people into the Navy you've got to start pulling them out, instead of commissioning new bases you've got to decommission bases. I was involved in a great deal of that.

Mr. Mason: What was the job sheet?

Admiral Johnson: It was to handle the policies of the Bureau of Personnel, to develop policies in accordance with the wishes of your seniors. Admiral Fechteler was the Vice Chief, Admiral Randall Jacobs was the Chief, and they were both splendid men with long experience in operations of the Bureau of Personnel. Of course, I had an awful lot to learn.

I think one of the most interesting parts of that job is

the relations with Congress. You are the Legislative Officer for the Bureau of Personnel; you are the one who must be the intermediary with Congress, who must present bills to Congress and clear them through the necessary committees.

Mr. Mason: You didn't operate through JAG then?

Admiral Johnson: No, we had one man in JAG who was also an excellent one -

JAG also had a representative to Congress and he and I went together to these things most of the time - Ira Nunn, a perfectly wonderful man, also with a great sense of humor.

We were, at this time, thinking of what we were going to do about postgraduate education. I was sent out by the Vice Chairman of the board to find a new site for the postgraduate school. This morning I was over in the old postgraduate school here; my wife's father used to be in command of that school. But that was entirely insufficient in size to handle the Navy's problem, so we had to find a site and build a new postgraduate school.

Mr. Mason: This was in addition to sending men to MIT and other places?

Admiral Johnson: Yes, this was the line school.

The senior member of this board was Captain Spanagel, who

was the head of the Postgraduate School, but he had to be recalled for some very urgent problem a couple of days after we started off on this mission. I think there were nine of us in this plane. I believe we inspected nineteen possible sites throughout the United States. I was left in charge of this mission.

Mr. Mason: What were the criteria for an ideal site?

Admiral Johnson: It had to be of sufficient size, or sufficient size that could be developed, to handle the large number that they were going to send there. It was desirable that it be in a good climate. There should be an airfield there. There should be a naval base somewhere near there, and a hospital. We went to all these places and settled on California; we chose Monterey.

Mr. Mason: What were the other possibilities, do you recall?

Admiral Johnson: St. Mary's College was one, in California. Whidbey Island up in Puget Sound was one. Several cities along the Gulf Coast - Biloxi, Mississippi was one. I think there were two sites in New England - I've forgotten what they were now.

In the minds of all of us this California site was by far the best.

Mr. Mason: I would think so, a perfect gem of a location.

Admiral Johnson: I believe the choice was the most constructive thing that I ever participated in. I remember being shown around it and being told that we could have it at a very moderate price, by Mr. Morris, who was the President of the Corporation then.

Mr. Mason: There were buildings there?

Admiral Johnson: Oh yes, the hotel was there; we took over the hotel. And Mr. Morris told us that he had such confidence in that area that he wasn't going to make his money off the government in this sale; he was going to make it on selling land to the people who went to school there and would want to come back and live there later. And that's just what happened too; the place is dotted with homes of retired officers.

I had to make many many appearances before Congress trying to sell this idea.

Mr. Mason: How large a school did you contemplate at that time, for how many students?

Admiral Johnson: I think for about a thousand. I think it wound up with two or three times that many there.

There was an amusing thing about that -- Mr. Vinson was the

chairman of the House Naval Affairs Committee at that time; they had not combined the two committees, military and naval affairs. We had managed to convince Mr. Vinson that this was the place we should go. Ira Munn was very helpful in this, and Captain Spanagel did a great deal convincing the committee. All of us worked on it. We had a wonderful man named Beanie Adams, who was one of the officers to chose the site.

Beanie Adams was President of the American Council of Education, Provost of Cornell, and President of New Hampshire. There was a Congressman from Texas, Price, and he was very incensed that we were not going to put this down in Texas. Beanie was testifying this day, very smooth and bland, and Mr. Price got up and said, "I want to know why you're not going to put this down on the Gulf Coast. You know that's where it ought to be. Why aren't you going to put it there? Captain Adams, give me an answer to that." Beanie looked at him and said, "Sir, we found the climate of the Gulf Coast is not conducive to maximum intellectual activity." The Congressman sat down and Beanie sat down.

One other little item along that line -- The Senator from Washington, Senator Magnuson, was also terribly upset about this. He wanted it at Whidbey Island. He asked permission to appear as a witness before the House Naval Affairs Committee in opposition to the decision they were about to make. We told him why we were putting it down there. His statement was something like this, "Gentlemen, I want to tell you that you're making the worst mistake possible putting this down in Southern California in this country club atmosphere of Monterey. There's nothing but sunshine down there. It's going to make a bunch of softies and sissies out of them. That's not what you're trying to develop in the Navy. If you just put that up in Whidbey Island where the tides run fast and the wind blows strong, this will put hair on their chests, and it will make sailor men out of them." When he'd finished Mr. Vinson said, "Senator, I want to thank you very much for your kindness in coming over today to give us the benefit of your advice. But Senator there's one thing you've lost sight of. This is going to be the first shore duty for these young men, and it's going to be the lambing season, and I think the lambs ought to be born in pleasant surroundings. Good morning, Senator."

We knew we had it won then.

Mr. Mason: I take it that the opposition to the thing was not to the school itself.

Admiral Johnson: No, it was for political local interest.

Just at this time I was a member, too, of the so-called Holloway Board, of which my friend Jimmy Holloway was the senior member. He was at this time the officer in charge of demobilization. We had come up with this ROTC plan for the training of the officers of the future - that was principally my task in the BuPers, to sell that idea to Congress. I guess I was with it for six or eight months.

That was, I think, a wonderful plan. And it was one of the greatest privileges I ever had, the association with some of the presidents of the colleges that helped us - the President of Harvard, the President of Brown, the President of Williams, the President of Yale, the President of Missouri, the President of North Carolina - Frank Graham. They would always drop whatever they were doing and dash down to Washington to testify before these committees.

Mr. Mason: Quite a different atmosphere then.

Admiral Johnson: It's what makes me so sick now. It was just terrific; they were very anxious to have the ROTC units in their colleges and they thought we had developed a splendid plan, which I think we had. Beanie Adams was responsible for a lot of that.

Mr. Mason: Would you talk about the plan itself?

Admiral Johnson: It was to a measure the one we'd had before, but greatly expanded, and with more financial benefits for the lads who participated in it. It provided extremely carefully chosen officers as professors of naval science.

Mr. Mason: They were to have active faculty status?

Admiral Johnson: Yes, they were to have active faculty status.

I think we were going to set them up in forty or fifty colleges. The people would be chosen by nationwide examination. They could express their preference for the college to which they would attend. We couldn't always give them what they expressed. I think they had to express four choices, and we'd give them always one of those. As I remember it, their tuition was paid all the time, and they got some small amount - fifty or sixty dollars in addition to that.

Mr. Mason: How many young men did you anticipate being in this program at a given time?

Admiral Johnson: I think it was somewhere around four thousand.

Mr. Mason: And the course of study . . .

Admiral Johnson: As I remember, they had just drills the first year there, and then text book studies in naval subjects for part of the course for the next three years; it was a four year course.

Mr. Mason: Which coincided with the regular college courses?

Admiral Johnson: Yes, and they could be taking a number of their own electives, not all naval. They were preparing for what they were going to do when they left the Navy, if they did. They would be commissioned in the Navy when they graduated. My recollection is that they had to do four years.

The colleges were so cooperative and so anxious to have them; it's incredible that this change has come about.

Mr. Mason: It has changed because of the attitudes of the students themselves.

Admiral Johnson: Yes.

Mr. Mason: Since it is a subject now, was any consideration given at that time to the training of black boys?

Admiral Johnson: I don't think it was. I don't think it was ever envisioned that it would be disqualifying - someone being black. But I don't think a determined effort was made to go out and recruit blacks as is now.

We had a wonderful black advisor for the Bureau of Personnel at that time, with whom I traveled a great deal - he was a civilian.

Mr. Mason: Were there any negro officers?

Admiral Johnson: I didn't have a single one in the Springfield. I think I had one in the President Adams, but they were very scarce then. Certainly change was required and was needed there, and I'm glad it has happened.

I suppose you've heard of the first captain of a destroyer, a man who recently became an admiral. I think this story is accurate: It was through the wisdom of Admiral Smedberg, then the Chief of the Bureau of Personnel, that this officer had worked up to executive officer of another destroyer. We'd never had a negro in command of a ship at this time. His commanding officer thought very highly of him as did everybody on board, so Smedberg said, "This is the time to make this break. We've got a good man for it. Let's give him one of our newest and best destroyers." I think someone told me there were three hundred and forty-three men on that destroyer, and this one black man. He did a splendid job of it, and it did much to break down the prejudices.

Mr. Mason: Did you have any problem with the Congress in terms of this new ROTC program?

Admiral Johnson: No, they were all very pleased with it. As I remember it, we had very little difficulty with it. Mr. Vinson was again a tremendous help.

I remember one day -- it was the first time anybody had run against him in a long long time, something like twenty years, in his district. He'd gone home to campaign down there and everything stopped in Washington in the Naval Affairs Committee. It was a critical time; we wanted to get this thing done, so Admiral Holloway and I flew down to Macon, got a car, and drove over to Millidgeville out to his farm out in the country. We'd sent him a message, and got permission to come in. I remember he met us on the steps of the farm house, put an arm around each one of us, and said, "What kind of trouble are you boys in now?" We told him what the trouble was. He had one of his aides down there with him, and dictated a message to Congressman Pat Drury of Virginia, who was the number two there, and told him to get on with our work there. It all went through in a breeze then.

Two of the members who helped us the most were Colgate Darden of Virginia and Mr. Stirling Cole of New York. I soon learned that Mr. Stirling Cole had had some unfortunate experience with the Navy; I don't know exactly what it was. I think at first there was some hostility (I thought of this this morning when I went over to the Chapel). At this time someone suggested it might be a good idea to ask Mr. Cole to come down to the Naval Academy; he apparently had shown that he was not fond of the Naval Academy.

Mr. Mason: He wasn't on the Board of Visitors?

Admiral Johnson: No, Colgate Darden was.

I asked Mr. Cole if he and Mrs. Cole and their sons would come down and attend the Chapel service and look over the Naval Academy and have lunch. (This was while I was with BuPers.) And he said that he would, he'd be glad to. He and his charming wife and young boys came down, and the superintendent, whose aide I had been in the past, was very kind to them and had him stand on the steps of the Chapel to review the Midshipmen marching in. Then there was a parade of the colors down the aisle. We later went through Bancroft Hall. Then we went out to Tulip Hill and had lunch with my old China friends, Mr. and Mrs. Louis Andrews - delightful folks. We drove back to Washington. I drove up to his house and let them out. He got out of the car and thanked me and started away, and he came back and said, (he'd always called me Captain Johnson), "Felix, I think I know what you naval officers are talking about now. Thank you." He was our great friend from then on. He was a very able man.

He called me at home one night to tell me that at a late session of the Congress they had just put the final approval on the Holloway Bill. So I'm a great admirer of Stub Cole. He was from upstate New York.

Mr. Mason: During your period in the department, something very fine happened to you.

Admiral Johnson: Yes, indeed it did.

They had a very unusual selection board for flag rank. As I remember it now, a list of officers eligible for selection was sent to some seventy flag officers in the Navy, and each one of them was asked to pick, I think it was, eighteen officers from that list to be promoted to flag rank. This was a radical departure from the normal system of assembling the board of nine officers and assigning them the mission . . .

Mr. Mason: Where they can discuss these people together.

Admiral Johnson: Yes.

This was principally handled by the Secretary's office. I had nothing to do with sending it out. In fact, I did know that it was going on, but it was done very quietly, and so I didn't know what the details of it were.

I was fortunate enough to be one of those chosen in this system. I think there were something like eighteen straight line officers, and maybe nine or ten aviators that were chosen.

So you can see, it would depend to a great extent on how well you were known.

Mr. Mason: The selection board usually is how many officers?

Admiral Johnson: Nine officers.

Mr. Mason: And here you were having seventy.

Admiral Johnson: Seventy officers, yes. And they did not have the records available to them of these officers who were up for selection.

The nine officers in Washington sit down for weeks and comb

over the records of these officers who are up before them.

The records were not available to these officers. It was a one shot deal; it was the only time, I think, it's ever been done.

The reports came in and they were tabulated. Again, I think this was done in the Secretary's office; Mr. Forrestal was there then. They were tabulated and the ones who had the highest number of votes got in.

That's the reason I think I was so terribly lucky in that I had been in some jobs where I had had the opportunity of meeting some of the senior officers, such as the flag lieutenant in China and the aide at the Naval Academy. They were strategic spots.

Mr. Mason: You say that this was the only time that such a method of selection was employed. Was it not considered a success or was it merely because it was a wartime technique?

Admiral Johnson: I believe it was a wartime technique, and I know there was some resentment about it. I didn't resent it naturally, but if I hadn't been selected I probably would have been annoyed, believing that I would have had a better chance if these officers had had an opportunity to look at my record. On the whole I expect the conventional way is better.

It was interesting to see what a spread there was who made this. There was one in '21, and they went down through '15 -

the spread of these twenty-seven officers ranged from the class of 1915 to the class of 1921.

Mr. Mason: How many names were given to the officers?

Admiral Johnson: I think it was about four or five hundred. Many of them were people who had been passed over before, though. I would say that of the active new field say there were probably one hundred and fifty men. But there were a number a pick-ups from the old field.

So this was a wonderful thing that happened to me. Admiral Denfeld had become the Chief of Personnel at this time. He was probably more learned in the field of Personnel than any officer I've ever known.

Mr. Mason: Tell me about Admiral Jacobs; he was there so long.

Admiral Johnson: He was there a long long time, and I did not have as close associations with him as I did with Admiral Denfeld because he left not too long after I got there. But I found him very easy to work with. Bill Fechøteler was the number two and it was through him that I had my most intimate associations with the top officers - he was splendid.

Then Admiral Denfeld called me one morning and said, "Sit down so you won't fall down." So I sat down and he said, "You're leaving."

Mr. Mason: How long had you been there?

Admiral Johnson: About a year and a quarter or a half. I don't seem to stay long places.

Mr. Mason: They bounced you around.

Admiral Johnson: And he said, "You're going to be the Director of Public Relations."

Mr. Mason: This was something of a shock, wasn't it?

Admiral Johnson: It was a tremendous shock.

Mr. Mason: Something you wanted to resist?

Admiral Johnson: Yes, I didn't like Public Relations very much. No, I thought I was doing fine over there and enjoying it very much.

Mr. Mason: Was this connected with your elevation?

Admiral Johnson: It probably was, yes. However, that has always been a rear admiral's job since then - the assistant for Plans and Policy.

Mr. Mason: But up to that time it hadn't?

Admiral Johnson: Up to that time it had been a captain.

Mr. Mason: Before you leave that assignment, were there any other aspects of it which are worthy of note?

Admiral Johnson: I think they were very wise to bring in Admiral Denfeld just before the end of the war when there were going to be such tremendous complex problems - personnel problems. He had more experience in personnel than anybody else. I think they were very wise to bring him in.

Admiral Jacobs went to a battleship group in the Western Pacific, and then he became Com 14 after that.

Mr. Mason: How did you plan for demobilization?

Admiral Johnson: This was Holloway's largest problem - by visiting every naval district, establishing there demobilization organizations which would supervise demobilization in that area under rules which were set up by and stemming from the Bureau of Personnel, and training the people in it. This was all done some time before the war was actually ended, before Hiroshima, so they were ready to go.

Mr. Mason: And did they build in this terribly important factor -

bring the boys home aspect of things, in their planning?

Admiral Johnson: Yes, they did. That was one of the biggest things in their plan - establishing bringing them home, the means of bringing them home . . .

Mr. Mason: The precipitous way in which public opinion demanded it?

Admiral Johnson: I'm afraid we were trying to slow down public opinion all the time, so we wouldn't have to do it so precipitously.

We had just about every ship that could possibly sail going back and forth across the ocean.

Mr. Mason: This is the Magic Carpet?

Admiral Johnson: Yes, the Magic Carpet bringing them home.

We had to establish very strict rules - the points which one was allowed for the time that he had in, the sea service that he'd had, the combat service that he'd had. We had obtained approval from the committees of Congress for the rules that we had to establish and the order in which people would be let out. This Chairman told us under no circumstances was there to be any departure from this rule.

The next week I got a telephone call saying they wanted

this young man out, they wanted him out right away -- from this same Congressman.

Mr. Mason: Were you tactless enough to repeat his . . .

Admiral Johnson: I was. I said, to him, "Mr. Chairman, you remember just last week you told us we would make no departures in this at all." He said, "Don't give me any of that stuff. I want this man out and I want him out day after tomorrow." So we had to do it.

As a result of that - I had a call another day from another Congressman wanting his young man out - an officer this was. He wanted him out right away. He was on a ship in Seattle and was sailing the next day for the Orient, and his time wouldn't be up until he returned the next time - that's when he normally would be let out. So he said he wanted him out right away. And I protested, and he said this was an officer --- and listen, I want this man out right away. I'm afraid I gave in again and sent a dispatch to the captain of the ship.

Within an hour I had a call from the young officer and he said, "I want to know what in the hell is going on. Who is this Congressman that's getting me out?" I said, "Your father is a powerful man politically, and that's the way they do it." And he said, "Will you tell my Congressman and my daddy to keep their damn hands out of my business. I'm sailing in this ship tomorrow, and I'll get out when my time comes and not before."

And that was a reversal . . .

Mr. Mason: Yes, and you had to impart this information to the Congressman.

Admiral Johnson: With pleasure. And he subsided.

Mr. Mason: How do you explain the fact that sensible men who have the total picture presented to them and understand the wisdom of the total picture succumb to this pettiness?

Admiral Johnson: I think much of politics is like that. It's based on self aggrandizement and what is all right for somebody else isn't good enough. I found this in some of them, not nearly all of the Congressmen, of course, but I found it in some of them.

Mr. Mason: But what does this do to our system of government - when all these exceptions come about?

Admiral Johnson: It concerns me very much. There aren't too many exceptions. I've quoted two cases; I don't suppose I had more than a dozen or twenty, or something like that.

There are so many fine ones up there that I don't want to cast any aspersions on the rest of them, but there are some who are small men inside and will do anything for political aggrandizement.

In general my relations with them were very rewarding and satisfactory.

Mr. Mason: In general, the Navy and the other services were not able to keep the lid on too tight, were they, in terms of demobilization?

Admiral Johnson: That's a very small percentage of the hundreds of thousands that we had, so I think we kept it going pretty well, and I think it was very fairly run.

Interview No. 5 with Vice Admiral Felix L. Johnson, U.S. Navy
(Retired)

Place: His residence in Leonardtown, Maryland

Date: 10 February 1972

Subject: Biography

By: John T. Mason, Jr.

Mr. Mason: It's certainly pleasant being with you two today. Last time you concluded by relating the fact that you were a fresh-caught rear admiral and that you had been selected to head up the Navy's public relations, and this was in the year 1946.

Admiral Johnson: Yes, in the late fall of 1946 I did move over from Assistant Chief of the Bureau of Personnel for Plans and Policy to this new assignment, which was over in the Main Navy building. I think I was tremendously fortunate in this job in having two such wonderful bosses. In the Navy system, in public relations you really have a civilian to whom you are accountable and a military man, to whom you are accountable, too.

The military man was Nimitz. As you see here, I have them alongside each other on my wall.

Q: Nimitz was Chief of Naval Operations?

Adm. J.: He was Chief of Naval Operations, and Mr. Forrestal was the Secretary of the Navy at that time. This was before he became Secretary of Defense - before the Defense Department was established. That happened during this time and a great deal of my work was somehow related to this pending change.

Q: What, may I ask, was the Navy's attitude toward public relations in that time?

Adm. J.: I think the Navy had a very healthy respect for the effect of public relations and gave it wonderful support. I never had anyone turn me down when I asked them to go somewhere to make a speech. For instance, particularly on Navy Day, we'd probably have 100 flag officers out making speeches all over the country. I never had any difficulty with any of them. They were very, very helpful, indeed, all the rank was.

Q: This was just the postwar period and prior to World War II the Navy was the silent service - known as the silent service - which more or less indicates their attitude toward public relations.

Adm. J.: I think that attitude had changed. Actually, I had no experience whatsoever in public relations. I've never been able to understand quite why I was shifted to this assignment. I didn't enjoy it as much as many other assignments I've had but I think it was a very instructive one for me. I learned a great deal from it, and I met a great many people - lots of civilians. I met a great many more civilians than I had ever met before. I knew all the Navy League people very well. They were a great help to the Navy.

One thing that was developed at this time - I think it had been started just before I got there and I continued it and expanded it - was something called the Secretary of the Navy's cruises for civilians. We would issue invitations to a group of civilians, usually from 12 to 20 of them, and invite them to make a cruise in a man of war. Usually it was a ship transiting the Canal, going from the West Coast to the East Coast, or a ship going down to the Caribbean for a shake-down cruise. We almost always had a group of civilians on board.

Q: What was the criterion for their selection?

Adm. J.: This was very interesting, too, because I made some changes in that. At first, it was only people who were very important in civil life - the heads of companies, the presidents of companies or very wealthy people who were selected. Then we began to see that we weren't reaching America as we wanted to, so we began to send a large number of educators on these cruises.

Q: And this was your idea?

Adm. J.: I'm not sure. Perhaps it was there before I came. I had to develop it, but I don't think that I thought up the idea. I believe I did do this: we began to take high-school people, too. A great many of them and even some elementary-school teachers would go along because we felt that the word about the Navy should be told to young America as well as to old America. This was very helpful. We got some marvelous letters from people who had gone.

One feature of these that I liked was that on each cruise an hour or so was set aside when these guests of the Secretary had the opportunity of going down into a compartment in the ship and talking with the assembled crew there, without any officers there. This was to give the enlisted men a chance to say whatever they wanted and so that the guests could get the average picture, instead of the sort of gilded picture, of the Navy. That helped a great deal.

Q: How were these educators selected?

Adm. J.: We asked the commandants of each district to supply us with a list of names and, with some guidance from us, as to the type of people we wanted. We'd say some Navy League people, some high-school teachers, some elementary-school teachers. But they were actually chosen by the commandants of these naval districts.

Q: How many people would be accommodated in a year, say?

Adm. J.: Oh, I suppose we'd run something like 5,000 through.

Q: A considerable number!

Adm. J.: Yes, it was.

Q: And the Navy stood the expense of this?

Adm. J.: I believe it did, yes.

Q: Did you also have conducted tours for congressmen and the like?

Adm. J.: We were always happy to have a congressman, and I have conducted a tour for them myself. I remember taking a group down to the Caribbean for the war games one year. I remember that among them was Senator Byrd of Virginia, who was very strong on economy.

Q: Harry Byrd, yes.

Adm. J.: Harry Byrd. I had this group of senators and congressmen on board the Missouri, and we showed them target practice in which the 16-inch guns were fired. There were very few - I suppose about six or seven shots were fired. Senator Byrd afterwards asked me what did each round cost that you fired this morning. I hadn't the foggiest idea what it cost, and I remember his telling me that he wanted the answer to that question before tomorrow morning. I worked most of the night getting it! But he was very fair and a very fine man. He helped the Navy a great deal. Of course, he was the brother, I believe, of our Admiral Byrd.

Q: Yes.

What other programs were sponsored by public relations at that time?

Adm. J.: We had speaking programs in which the commandants were encouraged to invite, to invite invitations, if you can use that expression, from the schools to ask the Navy to supply a speaker. We encouraged this throughout all of America. The officers serving on the staff there were required or told that we wanted them to make talks to these school children, also to colleges, and, not to conceal things about the Navy, but to try to present a true picture of the Navy to the civilian world.

I thought that was my mission in life, to make as many people understand the Navy as we possibly could, and present the Navy to them in the best light we could.

Q: Did you in this endeavor use the vast number of newspapers in the country, especially the weeklies?

Adm. J.: As I remember it, we had a meeting in my office once a week to which all the newspapers in Washington were invited to send representatives. They, too, were taken on cruises. I can't remember our relations with papers and magazines that were not located in Washington.

Did you ever hear of J. Walter Thompson and Company? They were advisers to us at that time. There was a man named Sam Meek - Samuel Meek. I've noticed by the way that he's apparently a tower of strength in the Episcopal Church. He's on the General Council. He was our adviser, and we had him come down - he was J. Walter Thompson's public relations representative. He came down and was shown through our office and spent, I think, about a month there going through all of our actions and he made recommendations to us as to actions which we should take in dealing with papers through the country. We pretty nearly followed his advice.

I remember once I went with him and a group of Navy League people to San Francisco to visit the Eleventh Naval District, just to look at a naval district with which they were not familiar. I had just taken over this job and had to make a speech the next week to the first classmen at the Naval Academy. I told Sam my problem, knowing so little about it, and he wrote a speech for me on the plane going out. He gave me a number of points to cover, which was very helpful and helped me put it over.

Q: May I ask a question? Was that an unusual procedure, to invite a Madison Avenue outfit to advise?

Adm. J.: Yes. This firm was hired by the Navy to do this. It was a commission they had from the Navy. It's a well-known reliable public relations firm and they were to scrutinize what we were doing and tell us what they thought we were doing right and tell us what they thought we were doing wrong.

Q: You mentioned a short time ago about Mr. Meek helping you with a speech you had to make at the Naval Academy. You now have in your hand an anonymous letter which was incorporated in this speech. Would you read it into the —

Adm. J.: This was incorporated in this speech, at his suggestion, and I think it was the thing that made the speech a success, as I felt that it was.

This is an anonymous letter written to the Bureau of Personnel, Navy Department, Washington, D.C., dated 16 March 1944:

Sir,

I am a survivor. I am a survivor from a destroyer sunk in Old Ironbottom Bay in the South Pacific. I'm glad to be alive. I don't want anything except to go on living and maybe when I get well again to go back down there and finish what we started. But, in the meantime, I have a story to tell, not about me, but about a ship, a grand little ship and her skipper. That ship lived. It lived and breathed and had a soul, just the same as any human being. Its spirit goes on living and will go on living forever and ever and its soul and spirit is that of her skipper. The ship has since been lost but the skipper of whom I speak had gone. He'd left us just three short weeks before, and when he left there were 200 men and officers on topside to see him off and not a word was spoken, the most eloquent tribute to the grandest shipmate a fellow ever had. You see, the skipper gave birth to this ship. He was a tall, gaunt westerner with a softspoken voice and a smile that made you feel like one of his best friends. But his eyes flashed hell fire and brimstone if you let him down. He gave his soul to that ship. She absorbed his quiet dignity, his strength, and character, and when she was attacked she fought with his hell fire and brimstone. With him on board, the ship was a living body and soul. Without him she was an empty shell. When he went over the side for the last time on that unhappy day last October, it was as though he took some vital part of each of us with him, as if the living soul that made her the grand old craft she was had curled up and died and let her spirit wither and her body tire. He'd had her through a year and a half of hell on earth. He'd fought the German U boat in the North Atlantic. He had pushed her through days and weeks of the cruel winter gales that howl down through the Denmark Strait. He'd kept our interest and loyalty up through months of the worst kind of operations, far from home, when food was scarce, when there was no mail, where liberty meant walking through snow and mud, maybe once a month to sit for an hour in a cold Nissen hut. Still, we had our ship, our snug little ship, and we had our skipper.

Then came Pearl Harbor and they needed a good ship to help lick the Nips, and so we went west. There, we hit the works, big and little, above the clouds, in the air, on the surface, and under the sea. After Tokyo with Jimmy Doolittle, the fringe of the Coral Sea action, then Midway, then through the entire Solomons campaign, shooting, hunting, fighting, screaming, fueling, working our hearts out and glad to do it because up there on the bridge, getting thinner and thinner and grayer and grayer, was our grand old man guiding our destiny, cheering us on, keeping our hearts busting with pride in the way he fought her, the way he handled her, the way she answered his every whim. And through it all, through all the battles, never a man was hurt. Oh, there'd been some close ones all right, but, God, the way he'd charge in, parry like lightning, and dash out, using her like she was designed to be used, for quivering, high-speed lance, and there upon her director were a beautiful painted tokens of his fighting and organizing skill, pictures of two enemy subs, one Nazi, for which he never got credit except from us - we knew, one Jap sub, which was recognized by the task force commander. Then there were nine Jap flags representing all the hell and havoc we gave the Nips on Tulagi, Tanambogo, Tavutu, Makimbo, and Guadalcanal in the Solomons. 111,000 miles of ocean he pushed us through, two shiploads of ammunition, three major battles, many many minor engagements, literally hundreds of beautiful maneuvers, making landings, fueling at sea, messenger service, passing mail and personnel and supplies under way, all in about 17 months of high-strung exciting adventure.

That, my friend, is service, and perhaps it wouldn't be so remarkable if you hadn't lived aboard this sweet little ship that gave us that service and with the man that made her tick. Teamwork, organization, skill, and, above all, pride, unspeakable, unbounded pride and joy throbbed in her very vitals. You don't have that without a leader, a hell-for-leather, God-fearing leader. My friend, we had the original.

So, then he left us. He was a sick man. His body

was sick but his spirit and soul never let any of us down for one second. So he had to go, and his eyes were red and so were ours as we helped him over the side into the little boat that took him away, and the last picture we had of him was his tall, straight body, stooped a little in pain, standing there in the cockpit of the gig, smiling through his tears with that warm smile that said you were his personal friend.

I'm just a small cog in this big machine, but for going on two years I served in the grandest ship and worked for the greatest skipper this Navy has ever had and I think you ought to know about him.

(Signed) A Survivor.

This was a letter which was received in the Bureau of Personnel while I was there, and from dates that he mentioned in there we were able to determine what ship he was talking about. It was the USS Monssen, a destroyer, and the captain, his beloved captain, was at that time Lieutenant Commander, later Vice Admiral Roland Smoot.

I used this in my talk to the midshipmen and ended by saying that there were many measures of success in this Navy life of ours, rank attained, high positions held, decorations you might win, but if none of those ever came your way and you had a letter about you written like this, then you are a success. That seemed to be very well received.

Well, I enjoyed my time in public relations.

Q: How long were you there?

Adm. J.: I think it was about 18 months.

Q: Before you go on, let me ask you a question or two about it. Did you have anything to do with combat art?

Adm. J.: Yes, we did. We had a great deal to do with combat art. We had a section in public relations which handled combat art. Walter Karig was stationed in our office. He's the historian who was writing a history for the Navy at that time. We had the Division of Naval History of which Judge Eller was the head. Judge Eller's assignment was what was then called Public Information. Public Relations was the all-embracing term. Public Information was a subsidiary unit. Naval History was one, and Civil Relations was one. Combat Art was a separate section, I think. We had a very large collection of works that had been done during the war by noted artists, many of them, and we had at least one - I think we had more than one - trailer in which these were mounted and which went around the country having exhibitions in various cities.

Q: Were you tied in in any way with publicizing the Navy for recruiting purposes?

Adm. J.: Yes, we were tied in with that, too. I can't remember exactly how now, but I think the recruiting officers had a period of indoctrination in Public Relations before they went out in the field, and we were constantly preparing suggestions of things for them to use in discussions with prospective enlistees.

It was quite a big, all-embracing job, Public Relations.

Q: Did you get involved with movie-making or anything of that sort?

Adm. J.: I think we did. I don't remember the details now, but I know I met quite a number of rather highly placed movie producers.

Q: What about naval museums? Were they under your hat, also?

Adm. J.: I don't remember. I'm sorry.

Q: Because they are now under the Director of Naval History.

Adm. J.: They are now, yes. The Director of Naval History certainly came under us and I expect the naval museums were a part of the same assignment. I would suggest that Eller would be the one who would know the most about this.

Q: Since you worked for a Navy and a Civilian head and they were two very contrasting personalities, you might talk about their attitudes towards public relations.

Adm. J.: It certainly was different. I believe that of the two, I preferred working for Admiral Nimitz, but I enjoyed Mr. Forrestal, too. He was a terrific man. He also had a keen perception with regard to public relations. Whenever his aide went away, on leave for anything, he required me to come up and sit at a desk just outside his office - or in his office, just outside the door to his inner office - to be right there to answer questions on public relations if they came up. He wanted to be able to hit the buzzer and get me to come in so he had the answer right away on anything to do with public relations. He was very conscious of its importance. He was a very remarkable man.

Q: Can you tell me something specific about him in that period of association?

Adm. J.: I traveled with him a few times. I remember going to Chicago with him once and going to New York with him once. Actually, I think he was a little bit shy. You wouldn't think so, but I think he was. He forced himself, I felt, to do everything possible to further public relations in the Navy. I don't believe I can remember that he liked to write his own speeches and he didn't want to be bothered when he was writing a speech. I can remember that he would say that he was going to be working on this talk that he was going to give at the National War College, or something, and I'd go back outside. This was when I was serving as his public relations aide as well as the Director of Public Relations. And something would come up that I thought was very important and I'd push open the door a little and he'd say, "Get the hell out of here. I'm busy on this important thing and I can't be bothered."

Admiral Nimitz was just wonderful. He was a marvelous man, very kind and understanding, strong, great sense of humor, a wonderful succession of stories that he knew. I told you that I had met him earlier down in Australia and formed a great admiration for him. I remember the day that he retired and the same thing was done for Mr. Forrestal the day that he left the Navy to become Secretary of Defense. Before they left their offices, we had lined the rail with officers, civilians, and enlisted men, all the way from their office down the corridor, down the steps, and out to the car at the entrance. There'd be an officer, a civilian, and an enlisted man, probably several hundred. The most side boys I ever saw anybody have. I don't remember who advanced this idea. Someone in the Bureau of Personnel suggested it, but it was easy to see that they were both greatly touched.

One other incident about Mr. Forrestal shows that neither he nor any of us realized what an enormous structure the Department of Defense was going to be. I heard him say that it was his desire that it would be restricted to 125 people. There would be, as I remember it, 9 or 15 officers in the Office of the Secretary of Defense and the rest of them would be laborers in the vineyard and secretaries. You see what it has developed into.

Q: This implies a different concept of the organization?

Adm. J.: It certainly does, an entirely different concept. My feel is that now - intelligence, for instance. I think intelligence is mostly done in the office of the Secretary of Defense. There was no contemplation at all at that time of having a Defense Intelligence Agency, and yet when that was set up there were in Naval Intelligence 1,125 people, and to establish the secretariat for the Defense agency it was necessary to send somewhere between 500 and 600 of these from Naval Ingelligence over to the Defense Intelligence Agency. Army and Air did the same thing. And those people who moved over to the Defense Intelligence Agency put so many requirements on their old offices that in less than a year they had to have more than they'd had when this thing started. It's really almost unbelievable.

Q: Has it bettered the system of gathering intelligence?

Adm. J.: I haven't served there with Intelligence, but I rather doubt it. I think we had very close relationship with Army,

Air, Navy Intelligence, and CIA, FBI. There was an FBI man in my office, a CIA man in the office, and we had other men over there. I don't know that it's better.

Q: Can you recall anything specific about Admiral Nimitz at that time when he was CNO?

Adm. J.: I don't believe I can, except that he was just universally beloved and admired by all of us. I never heard anyone criticize him in any way.

He didn't really like to make speeches but he would do it any time we asked him to. We tried not to ask him very often.

Q: Did you supply men with speeches when they were sent out?

Adm. J.: Yes, we did. We had a number of speechwriters in the office.

Q: Were these newspapermen or what?

Adm. J.: Most of them had newspaper background, yes. They were Navy people, but Reserve officers who had had some newspaper background. Some of them were darned good, too.

Q: In that way you kept control over what was said?

Adm. J.: Yes, you could keep control of a lot of things - or at least you could suggest it to Admiral Nimitz or to Admiral X, Y, or Z, but he didn't have to follow our advice. We suggested something that might be used but there was never any requirement that they use it.

Q: Did you have any role to play in the development of testimony before congressional committees?

Adm. J.: I think we did have some role to play on the subject of testimony establishing a Department of Defense, but not anything else that I can remember.

Q: Tell me about that, it being of particular importance.

Adm. J.: Well, the Navy was supporting having a Department of Defense and an extraordinarily able man, this Number Two up here, Forrest Sherman was the man who was in charge of the Navy's case in this. He did the liaison with the Hill and he did it magnificently. I believe I think that he is one of the ablest, brightest people I've ever met and look on him as a most terrible loss.

Q: When naval people were giving testimony before congressional committees on whatever subject, they had to be briefed in advance, didn't they?

Adm. J.: Yes.

Q: Was this the duty of the Public Relations Office?

Adm. J.: No, I think that was done by Admiral Sherman's office. He was, I believe, a special assistant to Mr. Forrestal for this mission, probably to Admiral Nimitz, too. I think he did the briefing. It's been so long my recollection may be wrong.

Q: Admiral Nimitz during World War II was something less than enthusiastic about providing the press with publicity on various naval engagements and the like. He did open up when he became CNO?

Adm. J.: I think when he became CNO he realized that it was incumbent upon him to furnish this information, advice, guidance, to the people who were going to deal with the press and to the press themselves.

Q: Was this changed attitude on the part of the Navy in the postwar period related in any way to the remarkable agility of the Air Force in publicizing its actions?

Adm. J.: I rather expect it was. I think we probably realized that we were being left at the post on publicizing our Service and it was essential that we do something about it.

Q: Did public relations have a kind of a manual, in your time there, for the use of men on board ship? I mean in dealing with various problems that pertain to publicity.

Adm. J.: I don't think we had any such thing.

Q: Would this not have been a fruitful area?

Adm. J.: Yes. It would have been very useful. I think we tried to handle that by having quite often - maybe once a quarter - a public relations conference in Washington, which would usually last four or five days, in which all features of public relations would be discussed with these public relations officers who were brought in from all naval districts and from the major commands at sea. They would spend, in many cases, up to a week and then they were expected to go back and assemble the public relations poeple from their minor commands, individual units, and communicate the same business to them.

At this time I would like to stress that Public Relations was in the market for any good ideas at all. They were all encouraged to - actually, I think this combat art traveling theatre arose in one of those meetings.

Q: The public relations organization throughout the Navy was fairly well developed then?

Adm. J.: It was indeed.

Q: All the major units – ?

Adm. J.: They all had public relations officers on the staff. Of course, we tried to stress, too, that there's such a thing as internal public relations as well as external public relations. This is a part of every commanding officer's duty.

Q: Would you elaborate on that?

Adm. J.: Well, I think that all the officers on the ship must be made aware of their public relations responsibilities not only to the civilian world, but to their enlisted men on board. What can we do to make the Navy more efficient and to make it a happier Navy? Can we start with more athletic events than we have been having? Can we have sailing races? Can we have a baseball team in every division? Anything that we can do to make the junior people happier to be in the Navy. This is something that everyone was striving for. We put a great deal of stress on internal public relations.

Q: Did this extend to the preparing of enlisted personnel for foreign ports when they were about to visit there?

Adm. J.: Yes, it did. Each ship was expected to be briefed

on what was acceptable in that country, what that country was like, and the things that they would not like done, and what we could do to make friends for America when we went in to those ports - why we had to be on our good behavior when we were there, try if you possibly can to learn a little bit of the language just to make them feel that you're interested in them.

Q: This could be achieved only through the commanding officer of a unit?

Adm. J.: The commanding officer, and his going down through all of his people on board, yes.

But this has been going on for a long time in the Navy. I can remember visiting foreign lands earlier, when I was a lieutenant and a lieutenant commander, the captain or the executive officer or sundry officers telling us what they expected of us while we were in that country, insofar as making that country a friend of the U. S. was concerned.

Q: In achieving an end like that if the urging of it came from the Director of Public Relations in the Navy, did you not have to have some active liaison with the State Department?

Adm. J.: I don't remember having any active liaison with the State Department.

This turns my mind back to an incident that happened in

Marseille, in Southern France.

Q: When?

Adm. J.: This was in 1928, when I was a lieutenant. It brought home to me the dislike which some countries had apparently for all Americans, and I think it made me realize then what I tried to practice later -- why we must present our best face to them.

I was on the back platform of a streetcar in Marseille. I wanted to go out to the embassy. I was arranging transportation to China by Suez. And there was a very fine-looking, distinguished-looking Frenchman standing there. I remember he had striped trousers, a cutaway coat, wing collar, and black hat. He was just standing there with his cane, and I said to the conductor in my execrable French could he tell me, please, when we got to the American Embassy because I wanted to get off there, and, of course, my French was very bad, and this distinguished-looking Frenchman said to me, "Are you American?" in French. I said, "Oui, Monsieur." This car had just started, it was going slowly, but it had started. He poked the end of his cane against my chest and gave me a hell of a shove and knocked me off the car into the road. I rolled in the road and the car steamed off. This was the opinion of some Frenchmen at that time of Americans, and I don't think it was resctricted to Frenchmen either.

Q: A pretty graphic illustration!

Adm. J.: Isn't it!
Let's move on to the next assignment, I think.

Q: It was in 1948 that you became commander of destroyers in the U. S. Atlantic Fleet.

Adm. J.: Yes. I was detached from public relations, relieved by Admiral Eddie Ewen, a distinguished and wonderful man, a great athlete and an aviator. We had served previously together in Brazil.

Q: Do I gather that you were just as happy to leave that assignment?

Adm. J.: Yes, I was. That was not my happiest assignment.

Q: Why wasn't it? You have a very outgoing personality.

Adm. J.: Maybe not outgoing enough! There were a great many opportunities for misunderstanding. It was very instructive. It did me a lot of good. I needed it, I'm sure I did. I think everybody needs some instruction in it, anyway. One thing that we did I was proud of -- speaking of needing it -- was the large, large numbers of public relations officers or to some commanding officers who had the time when we could get them we did give a course of a week or something like that, with various people who were specialists in internal public relations, in combat art, or relations with Congress, or relations with the public. That was needed by them and I think it was a very worthwhile project.

Q: How did you assemble such a staff of instructors?

Adm. J.: Practically all of them were from within our own office. Each one would come in and talk about his specialty. Judge Eller would talk about public information and dealings with the press. Somebody would talk about combat art. Somebody would talk on every subject there was - history. Walter Karig would always talk on history. It's been so long that I don't remember the names of the people who were with me then, but it was a fine crew.

I remember Admiral Byrd coming back from the south pole and we had to handle his press conferences.

Q: That was a natural, wasn't it?

Adm. J.: It was a natural, but it was a difficult thing.

Q: Why?

Adm. J.: Admiral Byrd had had two or three members of the press with him down on this expedition. He didn't like them and they didn't like him, and in these press conferences they would do something like this woman was doing yesterday to make Mr. Haldemann look bad, by the questions they would ask.

"Isn't it true, Admiral, that you did so and so down there?" This was a very difficult situation. That's the most serious one that I can remember, the relationship between the press who accompanied him and Admiral Byrd.

Q: Why were they permitted then to get in on the act?

Adm. J.: Because we can't keep the press out of anything. You can imagine what it would do if we said everybody can come tomorrow but the representative from The Star! It's hard to take but you have to put up with it.

Q: Their goading was somewhat personal, I take it?

Adm. J.: Yes, it was.

Q: Would you comment on the need to have a concept of security as Director of Public Relations for the Navy?

Adm. J.: It's hard sometimes to reconcile the thought of being secure in your relations and telling everything that the press wants to know. It's a very difficult thing to know just what you should tell them. It depends to some degree on who the person is. There were some there that I felt I never held back anything on at all. The same thing when I was Director of Intelligence later. There were a few people like Hanson Baldwin, say, that I felt I could tell anything to knowing that it would never be abused. But others were not so secure.

Q: Jack Anderson types?

Adm. J.: Jack Anderson types, yes. At that time, it was Drew Pearson. Jack Anderson was an assistant of his at that time. I was not fond of Mr. Pearson at all, and naturally you're inclined to hold back from someone you don't like particularly. But you can't let your personal likes and dislikes get into it too much.

It is difficult to reconcile those two.

Q: Were there occasions when you could brief the press and tell them that this was off the record? Could you do that? Did you do that?

Adm. J.: I think I did on some occasions, and I never had that abused. Never, if I told them it was off the record. Yes, I do remember a few instances of that. They always lived up to it.

Q: How did you determine what was off the record and what could be on the record? Did you have to consult with Intelligence on some of these things?

Adm. J.: Yes, we did consult. But generally you would know what you could say and what you couldn't. Just ordinary sense of propriety would show you what you couldn't use and what you could.

Q: Did you have any close calls in this area while you were Director?

Adm. J.: I don't remember any. No. I remember a few times when some of our senior officers were very irritated at the way they had been quoted or misquoted by the press, but there's not much you can do about it when it's been said.

Q: A retraction has little value!

Adm. J: It wasn't the most enjoyable assignment I ever had. Actually, I think I liked naval intelligence much better. Later when I was assigned as Director of Naval Intelligence I remember someone commiserating with me and said they thought it was a horrible strain to put on a person, taking him from a job where you tell everything to a job where you don't tell anything!

Q: Tell me about your cruise in the Atlantic.

Adm. J.: That was all too brief. I was ordered from Public Relations to the assignment of Commander, Destroyer Force, U.S. Atlantic Fleet. As I remember it, at that time we had about 110 - 115, possibly - destroyers and about five tenders. My headquarters were at Newport in the repair ship Yosemite.

In preparation for that I went down and had a talk with Admiral Blandy, who was Commander, Atlantic Fleet, and many of his subordinate commanders. I went to Key West, to the Sound School, and studied. I had about a month briefings going around to various places. I learned about the reserve fleet of destroyers, how they were being handled. At that time, too, I had to get some information on how our reserve operated because -

Q: You mean personnel?

Adm. J.: Personnel, yes - because so many of our destroyers had nucleus crews made up entirely of Reserves who, in case of a crisis, would have gone aboard these destroyers that were in reserve.

I went up to Newport, and that was a delightful job. I loved Newport, wonderful people there. I like Yankees anyway. I had a very fine chief of staff, Captain Henry Crommelin, one of the four or five Crommelin brothers from Alabama. I only had him about five months, I think, and then I got another relief who was equally fine, Captain McCorkle, later Admiral McCorkle.

Both Henry Crommelin and McCorkle became admirals.

I made, I think, two cruises to Guantanamo and to Roosevelt Roads while I was commanding the destroyer force. I had one disaster during this assignment, a very bad error of judgment. I think I had been there about a year and one thing in the Atlantic you're always looking out for are hurricanes. You keep a very sharp lookout on them, but you don't want them to catch you in port or in an exposed place if you possibly can help it.

Shortly before I took over, a hurricane did come up the coast and didn't follow the predicted track, hit Newport, and damaged several destroyers. It did, I think, about a million dollars' worth of damage. No ships were lost, though. I'd been there about a year when a hurricane originated down in the Caribbean, came up the coast, and seemed to me to be following exactly the same path that the disastrous one had followed the year before. We were watching it closely and when it got as far as Norfolk, all the ships in Norfolk had gone out in the bay to anchor and ride it out there. I picked up all my destroyers from Newport and two or three tenders there and, I think, two cruisers and took them to sea so we would not be caught by this hurricane in port.

My advisers decided that we should run to the southeast to get on the outboard side of the hurricane. So we headed for Bermuda, and everywhere I went that damned hurricane went, too. Everywhere I went it would change its course, it seemed to me, without any meteorological reason in the world for doing so, and it caught me down near Bermuda, and it just beat the heck out of us. We didn't lose any ships and we didn't lose any men, but it was a very bedraggled task force that I brought back to port the next day.

The maximum wind in Newport had been 10 knots, while I was down there having around 100 to 120 knots. So you can't outguess it.

Q: What was the general purpose of the destroyer fleet in the Atlantic at that time?

Adm. J.: At that time we kept quite a number of our destroyers operating with the fleet and its subsidiary task forces at Norfolk. Maybe a division of destroyers or a squadron of destroyers would go down and operate with the major units of the fleet for four or five months. Then it would be relieved by another unit of destroyers from Newport, and come back up there for regrouping, retraining, rearmament. Also we kept some in the Mediterranean. I think there were two squadrons we kept in the Mediterranean operating with the Sixth Fleet. And we were always available for crisis calls. We were training, training, training all the time, getting them ready for active duty assignments.

We also operated I would say about fifteen or twenty destroyers in support of the Reserve organizations. We supplied the ships for them to train on and for them to man when they went to sea for training exercises.

Q: This was pretty seasonal, wasn't it?

Adm. J.: Yes, throughout the summer, spring, and early fall, so it was seasonal.

I was raised in destroyers. I joined my first one, the Stewart, when I'd been out of the Naval Academy about a year and a half, and I suppose I served in seven or eight of them. This one here is the Lang, my first command. I commissioned her as her captain and had the honor of flying the President's flag in that picture because President Roosevelt was twice a passenger - several times, on two cruises.

Q: Yes, you told me.

Adm. J.: So I loved destroyers - They've always been sort of the cavalry of the Navy, the light forces. You live very closely with your officers and men and you get to know them all much better than you can in a big battleship with 1,500 people on board. I think in those days we only had about 150.

I thoroughly enjoyed that assignment.

Q: A little while ago you spoke about the Reserve Fleet. Tell me a little about that. How many ships were laid up and where?

Adm. J.: Most of the destroyers were at Charleston. Some were laid up in Philadelphia. Quite a lot of cruisers and battleships were in Philadelphia. Boston had some. As I remember it, they were responsible to two people, the commandant of the district, who was charged with the preservation of these ships, and to the commander-in-chief of the active fleet, who has a unit on his staff looking after the reserve ships. They were charged with seeing that these craft could be put back into commission in the shortest possible time.

Q: What determined the laying-up of a destroyer, say?

Adm. J.: When the end of the war came we just had a lot more than we needed, so we picked, I suppose probably, the more recent ones and kept them in active service and the older ones were decommissioned. Some were kept in partial commission so that they could be put in very quickly - reduced commission, it's called. The object was to have them ready to get them back in shape just as soon as possible and at the same time prevent their deterioration, and to make a sufficient number of them responsible for the training of Reserves.

I think at the end of the war we probably had 500 or 600 destroyers, and probably something like 250 were kept in commission. That's just a wild guess.

But, as I say, I loved that assignment. I think we would have lived in Newport after retirement had it not been for our having this farm. I love New England. Did you ever visit the Clambake Club?

Q: No.

Adm. J.: The Clambake Club is an extraordinary outfit which has a not very palatial clubhouse out on the point, and they were kind enough to make me an honorary member while I was there.

Q: This is at Narragansett?

Adm. J.: Yes. They have wonderful food there, and I think it's about once a month they have an actual clambake. They have an official who's called the Master of the Bake. One of the members of the club is the Master of the Bake. They probably put a thousand clams piled up in heaps with stones all the way through, covered all over with seaweed, then cover that over with canvas, and build a fire down under it so the steam comes up and steams these clams - bakes these clams underneath there. And they have to dig down exactly at the right time. The Master of the Bake, I remember, when it's getting near the critical point, when you're going to sweep the canvas off, stands up and holds his hand up, looks at his watch, sniffs the clams, and down comes the hand, and off goes the cover.

Q: Drama!

Adm. J.: Yes. There's another delightful club there - two other clubs that were kind enough to always make the commander of the destroyer force an honorary member.

Possibly one of the greatest joys of being there - I never had the opportunity of going to the War College. It seems to me I was always being sent to some working job. I asked for it three times, but never got it. But being located so near the War College, my flagship was tied at the dock about a mile and a half from the War College, I could go down and listen to lectures - to the distinguished lecturers who came to teach the classes over there, and I went about once a week to the lectures. That was a great privilege. We had a tremendous head of the War College, a man I admired tremendously, Admiral Spruance. I never served under him but I did see him often in Newport.

I had a very short tour in DesLant. I think it was just about a year and a half.

Q: During that time were there any NATO exercises?

Adm. J.: I don't remember any, no. We had quite a number of exercises of our own. There was the Black Force and the Blue Force and the Red Force and the Green Force along our coast and down in the Caribbean. But I don't remember any NATO exercises.

Q: Any Latin-American navy cooperation?

Adm. J.: I don't think there was any, no. We would occasionally see a Brazilian officer who came to this country, someone whom I'd known down there, but not in connection with the destroyer force, particularly.

Q: Well, this other command was coming up and that's why it was such a brief tour?

Adm. J.: Yes. Naval Intelligence at that time was headed by Admiral Thomas B. Inglis, a wonderful intelligence man, a wonderful officer all around, and apparently they needed him at sea in the Pacific. So my friend Admiral Fechteler, who was Chief of the Bureau of Personnel or Assistant Chief, at that time, I don't remember which, called me from Washington and told me that he planned to detach me in about ten days to become the Director of Naval Intelligence in Washington and that I would be relieved by Admiral Wooldridge as ComDesLant. Admiral Wooldridge and I were roommates aboard the Delaware twenty or twenty-five years before, a very close friend of mine. I was honored to have him become commander of the Atlantic Destroyer Force.

Q: Yes, but you were reluctant to give it up?

Adm. J.: Very reluctant to give it up, yes. I think I was happier in that job than any other one I'd ever had.

Q: Now what made for that?

Adm. J.: Lots of ships, destroyers, delightful people, and it seems to me destroyermen have always been a special breed. I loved my association with them. I had such a fine staff. At this time McCorkle was my chief of staff because Henry Crommelin had been promoted and was down in the Caribbean, I think commander at Guantanamo.

So, we reluctantly packed up. I had my last clam at the Clambake Club and drove down to Washington. I had about ten days in which to take over and it seems to me I was rather intimidated by the noted people with whom I was going to be coming in contact. Admiral Inglis took me around to call on all the people with whom he associated.

Q: You mean within the organization or without?

Adm. J.: Within and without. Without to the extent that - well, Bedell Smith, for instance, over in CIA, and Mr. Hoover I'd never met, so I was introduced to Mr. Hoover. The Air Force Director, who was Pearre Cabell. The Army was - his first name was Alex but I can't think of his last name. I got to know all of them and, of course, I had to get to know the senior Navy people around Washington because we quite often briefed the Chief of Naval Operations and Op-03. Also, having the Defense Department then, I think it was once a week that the three of us went in to General Marshall's office and briefed him for about half an hour. The Secretaries had to be briefed, so there was quite a lot of that going on.

Q: Any White House briefing or anything?

Adm. J.: I never had to give one at the White House, no. I briefed his naval aide.

Q: Dennison?

Adm. J.: Bob Dennison and Jim Foskett were the two that I dealt with.

I very much enjoyed my relationship with the foreigners there. I hadn't had too much experience with the broad foreign population in Washington, but you see all of the Naval attaches. They in a way court you, I think. You're asked to so many dinners and parties you have to go out almost every night. And you have to have a lot of them to your own house. This was rather rough on my wife but she did it well and enjoyed it.

The next spring we had an intelligence conference in Frankfurt, Germany, and I went over with two aides, I think. This was a conference of Army, Air, and Navy intelligence, people from all over the world would come there and we put in about a week or ten days talking with them and listening to their stories of what they knew.

Q: These were U. S. representatives in various parts of the world?

Adm. J.: Yes. I visited England. It was the first time I'd ever been in England. It seems amazing that I should have been in the Navy that long. Of course, Germany, Holland, Sweden, Norway, Denmark, Switzerland, Italy, France, Portugal. I was gone about six weeks - three or four days in each of those talking to our naval attaches in all of these places, meeting their intelligence officers. We always asked them to come to talk with me when they came to Washington.

One of my first acts as Director of Intelligence, when I'd been there about a month, I invited the British Director of Naval Intelligence to come over to visit me and discuss various problems around the world.

Q: How frank a relationship did we have with the British at that time?

Adm. J.: Very frank indeed. I'm not sure that it is so frank now, but it was at that time. Rear Admiral Eric Longley-Cook was DNI at that time.

During my three years there I attended two of these conferences —

Q: In Frankfurt?

Adm. J.: — these Frankfurt conferences and had Admiral Espe, who was my Number Two, go to the third one.

Q: What was accomplished at an International conference of that sort?

Adm. J.: Well, we would try to get a picture of what the problems were in China, say — I'm not sure we had the man from China. I believe we had a special conference of the Asiatic countries in Pearl Harbor once a year. I didn't go to one of those, but Carl Espe did. But this permitted us to see how they were getting on in their country, what were the irritations, what were the pluses we had or the minuses, what dangers could they see or envision coming from this area. It was, I think, very helpful.

Q: Was it in a sense an estimate of the political situation and the currents in these countries?

Adm. J.: Yes.

Q: And how they affected the flow of intelligence?

Adm. J.: Yes. And also an estimate of the forces available to those countries. I think we still don't know too well just what Russia has got, and, of course, we were awfully anxious to find out more at that time.

I enjoyed my weekly meetings with Mr. Hoover every Tuesday afternoon.

Q: What was the purpose of that? All the directors of intelligence agencies?

Adm. J.: All the directors of intelligence agencies met with Mr. Hoover. This was to discuss intelligence problems within the country, internal intelligence problems. I think there are a lot of people appearing on television now that I would have been rather doubtful about had they been around at that time. It wasn't really spying on anybody. Each one of us was keeping the other informed as to what our problems were and asking for any help that we needed.

I was very fond of the air and the army intelligence officers. They were splendid.

Q: Who presided at those meetings? J. Edgar Hoover?

Adm. J.: Yes.

Q: Tell me a little about him.

Adm. J.: Oh, I think he was amazing, terrific. There was no doubt about who was presiding, all right. We all stood up when he came in and he sat down at the head of the table, and he went around the table asking each one of us what problems we had we felt ought to be brought up, then he would explain some of his own problems.

I had a very fine man from his office who was in my office at ONI, de Loach.

Q: He was liaison?

Adm. J.: Yes. He was the No. 3 in the FBI when he retired last year. I went to see him just before he retired. He went to Frankfurt with me. He was completely a part of our team. We had almost instant access to Mr. Hoover if we needed it, which we tried not to.

I also enjoyed equally, I think, sitting at the feet of Bedell Smith, who was a most remarkable character - General Smith. He was delightful. You remember he left that job to become Under Secretary of State. That was just after I had retired from the Navy.

I think that's about enough about intelligence.

Q: Oh, I think perhaps we could ask a few questions!

Adm. J.: All right. One more conference. We had a conference, I think it was once every ten days, which was attended by all the admirals in the Chief of Naval Operations office when we discussed intelligence problems of mutual interest. This was very helpful in keeping me in close touch with all of them. Sometimes it seems you're wasting time in so many conferences, but it's very difficult to talk to somebody unless you have served closely with them. You can let down your hair much more easily.

Q: Naval intelligence was the chief information-gatherer in the Navy at that time?

Adm. J.: Yes. There was not any Defense Intelligence Agency at that time. There was operational intelligence. Every admiral had an operational intelligence officer on his staff, but he is getting some of his briefing from his boss and getting a lot of it from us, too. I think it was once a week that we had all the heads of units in naval intelligence who came into my shop and we sat down and talked for a couple of hours about various problems and what was happening throughout the world. Was Larry Healey there when you were there? He was a great brain, a wonderful man. I have a card from him on the desk there now. He was terrific and writes beautifully. Unfortunately,

I made a big mistake. I would say that Larry was the No. 2 in the operational intelligence office in ONI. He worked for a captain there. We wanted the Secretary of the Navy to make a speech which had some intelligence application and I talked with the Secretary about it. He said, "Well, you get it written and I'll give it." I think it was to a congressional committee.

Well, Larry wrote it and I gave it to the Secretary and he gave it to the Congress. He sent for me the next day and said,

"The best speech anybody's ever written for me. I want that man transferred into my office. He'll be my speechwriter."

Q: Oh, you lost him!

Adm. J.: No, I didn't. I was quite intransigent about it. I was almost insubordinate, but I finally managed to talk him out of it. Larry was viewing it with horror, too!

Q: Who was the Secretary?

Adm. J.: Oh, dear, I don't remember now. He hadn't served in the Navy and hadn't had much contact with it at all. I don't remember his name now.

Q: Tell me about the appointment of attaches and that sort of thing in your time.

Adm. J.: An officer could write to me or to the Bureau of Personnel and request that he be assigned to the attache system, or we could ask for someone by name -- ask the Bureau of Personnel to let us have this man for attache to London or Paris or wherever it was. Quite often we'd get nominations by an admiral telling us that he thought Joe Doaks would make a fine attache and, of course, he'd met him there and he'd known something about Portugal.

I think we had in general a very fine selectivity of naval attaches. We had a personnel officer in ONI with several assistants and he was in immediate touch with the Bureau of Personnel at all times. He was over there at least once a week, going over prospective vacancies. I only had to remove one during my three years there and that was because of the activities of his wife. We had a fine crowd of attaches. But the wife of one of them was not behaving too well so we had to bring him home. But that's the only one.

Q: What was the concept of intelligence-gathering in that time? What was your purpose in ONI?

Adm. J.: I'm afraid that's rather difficult to put in a few words. Probably, my purpose was to be so familiar with what was going on throughout the world to ensure that nothing like

Pearl Harbor ever happened again, and to ensure that the United States made as many friends throughout the world as was possible.

Q: That's quite a difference, quite an advance from pre World War II times, when ONI was considered in many quarters to be a kind of a residual library or something, keeping records and keeping intelligence in books, monographs.

Adm. J.: I don't think we did very much of that in my time. They never showed them to me if they were there!

Q: Monograph-keeping was not a part of it?

Adm. J.: Yes, they did keep monographs. I didn't read too many of them, I'm afraid. I remember the confidential file that they keep on every officer there. I could never see mine. They wouldn't let me have my own record. I could see everybody else's in the Navy and they'd produce them very quickly, too.

Before any attache went overseas, before he was accepted for the system, we went over his confidential file very carefully and occasionally that resulted in removing that perons from consideration.

Q: What was the policy on preserving intelligence, using intelligence, making it available?

Adm. J.: I think it was through these weekly conferences we had with all of the OpNav admirals present, in which they were brought up to date on any changes in intelligence that we knew, and it helped guide them in some of the decisions they had to make.

Q: Was there an intelligence summary of any sort published? Did you circulate anything of that sort to qualified people?

Adm. J.: I would think we must have done it but I just can't remember. It would seem to me essential that it be done, but I don't remember it, the shape of it at all, or the section that turned it out.

Q: In your time, the situation in the Far East was getting hot.

Adm. J.: Let's see. That was 1952. I left in 1952. How hot had it got?

Q: Korea?

Adm. J.: Oh, yes, of course. I might tell you on Korea that this caught us very cold. It shows that we probably weren't doing our job too well. But we only had one intelligence officer in the Seventh Fleet - one, and there was an immediate need for a lot of them. So we rounded up sixteen from the fleet in Pearl Harbor and flew them out, and I went out myself the next day. With these sixteen the intelligence officer of the Seventh Fleet then had an adequate staff, which he handled very skillfully.

Turner Joy, the admiral out there, was my best friend in the Navy and I stayed with him while I was there - this was in Tokyo, and I flew over to Korea and spent about a week there and about another week in Pearl Harbor. We had had to round up quite a number of people from our own office to send out to Pearl to replace the people whom we had sent out to Korea.

Q: Were these people you sent to Korea language people?

Adm. J.: No. I don't think we had anybody who could speak Korean at that time, except possibly the man who was out there.

Q: Why the single intelligence officer with the Seventh Fleet?

Adm. J.: Well, the Seventh Fleet was of minute size at that time. Maybe it was not the Seventh. What was the one - ?

Q: The Seventh Fleet.

Adm. J.: Yes. The admiral was ashore and I think there was only one rear admiral in addition to Vice Admiral Joy. It was a very tiny task force because we just hadn't expected this thing to come along.

I remember flying over Inchon. It seemed the most incredible place in the world for a landing to be able to take place. I think the tide went out about two miles, and you had to catch it just in a few minutes and get the hell out of there before it went out again. Extraordinary tide! Something like the Bay of Fundy tide.

Was 1952 when Korea happened? That's when I retired. I may tell you about that.

I was keeping awfully long hours in the Pentagon. This was a very demanding job, really. I got there before eight every morning and I stayed till about 5:30, and got home just in time to dress to go out to dinner. So it was a very demanding job. And it isn't all social, this going out at night. You learned a lot, too. You make friends for the country and you learned a lot about people who will possibly come in and tell you things later that you need to know. So, it wasn't just fun, this social life.

I began to get arthritis very badly and I had several stays of a few days in Bethesda for treatments. I had a wonderful doctor on the intelligence staff, John Bachulus. I still get a Christmas card from him, too. He had such skillful hands that when I got tied up in a knot I'd ask him to come up to my office, and I'd flop on the couch, and within about ten minutes he had me back moving again. It was really amazing the skill and the healing touch of his fingers.

But, eventually, in the summer of 1952, it got so bad that I was sent out to Bethesda and stayed there for about six weeks. The doctors at that time said that I was going to be tied up with this for a long time, stooped over, I couldn't stand up straight. So eventually, after consultation, I decided that the best thing to do was to retire and with quite a lot of reluctance because I'd enjoyed it so much, but also with anticipation because I had this farm and I looked forward to living here. I talked with Admiral Hogan about it and he knew the case and thought that that was the best thing to do.

So on the 1st of September 1952 I retired, came steaming down the road with my wife. We had moved our things down from Washington a week or so before this. I had a perfectly marvelous time in the Navy, but I've had a perfectly marvelous time here, too.

Q: I can see. And it continues on!

One other question that does occur to me. Tell me about the relationship of ONI with the CIA. What kind of cooperation was achieved?

Adm. J.: We had a representative in CIA and CIA had a representative in ONI. We had a meeting in CIA once a week presided over by General Bedell Smith at first, and later by Allen Dulles. I think there was a complete mutual trust between these organizations. I never knew of any friction to arise between them.

You know that they have taken on that staff, CIA, a number of retired naval officers?

Q: Yes. They also took people who were at ONI, did they not, and attracted them over to CIA?

Adm. J.: Yes. I don't think they were attached to ONI any more. They were people who had had experience in ONI who were working for CIA. But there was one man over there who was still working for us, and one man with us who was working for them. Part of it was, I think, the excellent relationship which existed between the head of CIA, General Smith, and the heads of these other agencies. We all called him "General Smith." There was no doubt who was running the show. He was a very forthright, forceful person and available to any of us at any time. I admired him tremendously.

Q: Did ONI cooperate with CIA in some of their foreign operations?

Adm. J.: I just can't remember now. It seems to me that we did. You mean their under-the-table operations?

Q: Yes.

Adm. J.: We did, but it was something that you had to be terribly careful about because you couldn't have official government agents over there, which ONI men would be - you couldn't let them catch him going under the table. It would cause great difficulty between the two countries, but we did cooperate with them whenever they asked us to.

We haven't mentioned State.

Q: No. Do talk about State.

Adm. J.: We had very close relations with State, too. I can't remember the man's name. Park was his first name. (Park Armstrong). He was Assistant Secretary of State for Intelligence. We all liked him very much, and he sat in on these meetings with CIA and with FBI, too. I don't remember ever having any difficulties with him.

Q: Because of your close liaison with the heads of all these agencies, was there, in your opinion, any duplication of efforts in the intelligence field?

Adm. J.: I think there was. I think sometimes we would go through a long struggle to get a bit of information about Italy, maybe, have a man working on this in Italy, and just as he got it he finds that one of the other intelligence agencies has been working on the same thing and gone through a hell of a struggle to get it. This requires, of course, very close relationship between the attaches of the three services and of State in each country. But they generally worked together very well. I don't know of any critical duplication of effort.

Q: Did ONI sponsor any kind of intelligence school?

Adm. J.: Yes. We had one in Great Lakes and another one in Washington. I don't remember too much about the one in Great Lakes, but I was terribly proud of the one we had in Washington for the preparation of our attaches. As I remember it, it ran something like this.

We would decide a young lieutenant or lieutenant commander was going to an intelligence assignment. He'd be ordered to Washington. He'd have a few days in our office to get a general briefing. Then he'd go over to this intelligence school, where he was taught intelligence for three months - classes in every aspect of it. At the end of that time, he had made his choice or we had made it for him on the country to which he was going to be assigned, and then he was sent to a language school to learn the language of that country, and so was his wife sent to this language school. You've no idea how much that improved the reception given to these officers in the countries for them to arrive there speaking that language. Even if you are not absolutely expert, if you know enough to try, that makes a difference.

I told you about my Brazilian friend when I inspected a destroyer. That's an example of it.

Q: It seems like such an oversight for us to have gone on so many years without emphasizing this.

Adm. J.: Yes, it went on for many years. I think it was my predecessor, Admiral Inglis, who established the school there. But I was terribly proud of that, and seeing these young people all over the world as I traveled around, having the attache and the assistant attache there break into Italian or Swedish. We only taught one Scandinavian language. I was intrigued about that. We only taught Swedish. We didn't teach Norwegian.

Q: The reason for that being what?

Adm. J.: Swedish, our Scandinavian friends tell us, is halfway between Danish and Norwegian and it's just about as essential that you get along with the next country as it is with the country of those three to which you are accredited. So if you can talk Swedish, you can get along with both the others all right, and pretty soon you'll adopt the Danish peculiarities. I think Sweden was rather proud of that, that we taught only Swedish, but it seemed the Danes and the Norwegians had no objection to it.

I believe there were seventeen languages we taught at that school. Maybe twenty-seven, I'm not sure.

Q: I do want to thank you, Admiral, for giving me this time. It's been delightful meeting you and your charming wife. I've enjoyed every moment of the time spent with you.

Adm. J.: Dr. Mason, I'm so honored that you thought I had something that would be of interest of people in the future and have recorded it. I feel very modest and humble about it. I really do.

Index

for

series of interviews

of

Vice Admiral Felix Johnson,

U. S. Navy (Retired)

Adams, Dr. Arthur S. (Beanie): President of University of New Hampshire - President of the American Council of Education, p 206; influential in developing the Post WW II plans for ROTC, p 208.

Adams, The Hon. Charles Francis: serves as skipper of the Lambert yacht - ATLANTIC for the Spanish race of 1928 - invites Johnson to be his navigator, p 55, 58; instrumental in having Johnson become Flag Lieutenant to Admiral McVay, CinC Asiatic, p 66; present for the commissioning of the USS SPRINGFIELD, p 181, 184.

ASIATIC FLEET: (see entries under USS PENGUIN - and YANGTZE River Patrol) 2nd assignment of Johnson, p 53, 60; picture of life in the fleet, late 1920's - p 71.

WOLFE, Dudley: owner of the MOHAWK (private yacht) - invites Johnson to participate as his navigator, p 54 ff; rules of race prevented a professional from serving, p 55.

BAXTER, Dr. Phinney: p 118.

BEARDALL, RADM John R.: former aide to FDR - becomes Superintendent of the U. S. Naval Academy in 1942, p 131.

BEARY, VADM Donald B.: skipper of the DD SUMNER (1921), p 24-25.

Belknap, RADM Reginald: Skipper of the USS DELAWARE (1919), p 12, 14.

USS BOUGAINVILLE: p 200-201.

BRAZIL: Johnson goes to join the Naval Mission - 1934, p 86; duties, p 87; the Brazilian Navy, p 87-91; Brazilian customs, p 91; life in Rio, p 95-6.

Bristol, Adm. Mark: p 66-67.

BRYON, Lt. Comdr. Hamilton (Ham): skipper of the USS Paul Jones with the Asiatic Fleet, p 63-4.

BU PERS: Johnson detached from the SPRINGFIELD at Okinawa and returns to BuPers as Director of Plans and Policy (Pers A), p 198; p 202; Johnson represents BuPers before Congressional Committees, p 203; task of selecting new site for PG school, p 203 ff; Johnson's principal task to sell Congress the amended ROTC plan for officer training, p 207-9; BuPers and black officer advancement, p 210-211; plans for demobilization after WW II, p 218 ff.

BURKE, ADM. Arleigh: Origin of his designation as '31-knot Burke', p 146.

CARNEY, Adm. R. B.: p 48; Chief of Staff to Adm. Halsey - orders Johnson to the staff to serve as liaison officer between Halsey and Gen. MacArthur, p 150-1, p 156-7; Johnson's estimate of him, p 171.

USS CASTOR (ex-CHALLENGE) - general stores issue ship, p 113; Johnson takes command, p 115.

CHAMBERLAIN, General Steve: p 157.

CinC, SoPac: Johnson named as liaison between Halsey and MacArthur, p 151; first duty to master South Pacific picture, p 151, p 155-156; on first flight from Noumea to Guadalcanal seaplane catches on fire, p 152-3; reports to MacArthur staff on Dec. 21, 1943, p 156; future schedule as liaison, p 157-8; Johnson named as Naval Aide to Gen. MacArthur for the landing at Hollandia, p 159-165; after Hollandia

Johnson ordered home to command a cruiser, p 165.

CLAMBAKE CLUB: p 257.

COCOS ISLANDS: p 106; Johnson in DD LANG directed by FDR to make a survey of the islands, p 108.

Cole, The Hon. W. Sterling (STub): Member of Congress from New York, p 212-213.

DARDEN, The Hon. Colgate: helps with the ROTC plan in Congress, p 212.

DAVIS, The Hon, Dwight: p 70.

DD Force, Atlantic Fleet: Johnson assumes command, p 252 ff; involvement with Atlantic hurricane, p 253-4; training of reserves, p 254-5; the reserve fleet, p 255-6; fleet exercises, p 258-9.

DEERFIELD ACADEMY: p 119-120.

USS DELAWARE: first assignment for Johnson (1919), p 12; Adm. Belknap is skipper, p 12; loss of crew to postwar (WW I) retirements, p 13; recruiting in New England, p 13-14; staff officers, p 15; Johnson's duties on board, p 16; acts as troopship to withdraw U. S. Marines from Santo Domingo and Haiti, p 19-20.

DEMOBILIZATION - after WW II: p 218; rules established, p 219; Congressional deviation from the rule, p 219-222.

DENFELD, Adm. Louis: congratulates Johnson on ship handling, p 64-5. Chief of Naval Personnel, p 216.

ELLSWORTH, Ernie: Ensign on the BB TENNESSEE - wins sail boat contest in the fleet, p 83-4.

FECHTELER, Adm. Wm.: in command of naval forces at Hollandia landings, p 164.

FINCHHAFEN: one of the three landings in the Hollandia operation of General MacArthur, p 160-161, p 165.

FLETCHER, Adm. Frank Jack: p 110-111.

FORRESTAL, The Hon. James: SecNav (1946), p 237-239.

GRAHAM, Dr. Frank: President of the University of North Carolina, p 127-8.

HEALEY, Lawrence: Number two man in operational intelligence, ONI, p 266-7.

HOLLANDIA OPERATION: p 159; Nimitz supplies carrier coverage for MacArthur, p 159-160; Kinkaid furnishes the USS NASHVILLE as flagship for MacArthur, p 160; the General under fire on the beach immediately after the landing, p 163; p 164.

HOLLOWAY, Adm. James L.: as Lieutenant Commander he ran a secondary battery school on board the USS CALIFORNIA (1933), p 80-1. President of the Holloway Board, p 207-8; p 211.

HOOVER, The Hon. J. Edgar: p 260; meets weekly with the various directiors of intelligence, p 264.

ICHANG: on the Yangtze at foot of the gorges, p 29-30.

INTELLIGENCE GATHERING: how the new Dept. of Defense Intelligence set-up changed the picture, p 239-40.

Japanese NAVY: Observations on the Japanese Navy, 1929 - p 68 ff.

JOHNSON, Vice Admiral Felix L.: family background, p 1-4; promotion to flag rank, p 214.

JOY, Adm. C. Turner: Ordnance Officer, Mine Depot, Yorktown, Va. (1931), p 73, p 271.

KAMIKAZE: First experience with one at Hollandia, p 192; attack on picket ships, p 195; p 197-8.

KING ALFONSO: (1928) King of Spain comes on board the ATLANTIC and invites the party to dinner at his palace in Santander, p 59.

KINKAID: Adm. Thomas C.: P 158-9.

KOREAN WAR: need for intelligence officers, p 270-1.

Janada - a Brazilian fishing raft; p 96.

JONES, Admiral Cary: p 185, 191.

LAMBERT, Girard: President of the Lambert Pharmaceutical Company and owner of the racing yacht ATLANTIC, p 55.

USS LANG: Johnson commissions a new DD, p 97-8; first exit from New York harbor, p 99-100; escorts FDR on a cruise, p 101-3; joins the Pacific Fleet for exercise off Pearl Harbor, p 109-111, 113.

LAWRENCE, John Endicott: Johnson forms friendship with him as result of emergency landing in Pacific, p 152-4.

LEHRBAS, Col, Larry: Military aide to General MacArthur - former representative of NEWSWEEK in Shanghai, p 162-3, 165.

LOUDERMILK, Dr. Walter: taught forestry at Nanking University - 1921, p 34.

MacARTHUR, General Douglas: p 70; p 152; Johnson's first meeting, p 156; p 157-9; the Hollandia operation, p 159-165; his talent for leadership, p 168; his courage, p 169; the relationship of MacArthur and Halsey, p 168, 170-175.

MAGNUSON, Senator Warren: proposes Whidby Island as location for the New PG School, p 206-7.

MANUS: p 175-177.

MARSHALL, The Rev. Peter: his Pearl Harbor day sermon at the Naval Academy, p 129-130.

McVAY, Adm. Charles B.: Cinc, Asiatic (1929), p 65-66; calls on Gen. MacArthur, p 70.

MEEK, Samuel: PT representative from J. Walter Thompson agency to the Navy, p 229-230; writes speech for Johnson to be delivered at the Naval Academy p 230-1.

USS NASHVILLE: assigned as flagship for General MacArthur in the Hollandia operation, p 160-1, p 164.

U. S. Naval Academy: Johnson's appointment to the Academy, p 4-6; reduced course because of WW I, p 7; restrictions to Naval Academy life, p 8-10; training for diplomacy, p 21; Johnson returns (June, 1926) for teaching duties in the Navigation Department, p 41-42; p 44-45; 'saavy' sections, p 45-47; Academy standing, p 47-8; influence of Chapel services, p 50-53; Johnson ordered to Academy as Aide to the Superintendent and Secretary to the Academic Board (July, 1941), p 116; efforts at (and methods) of recruitment for the Academy, p 117 ff; Blue and Gold officers, p 121; the Board of Visitors, p 126-129; with advent of WW II problem of securing officers for Academy duty, p 130; p 132.

U. S. NAVAL INSTITUTE: Johnson invited to become Assistant Editor in 1926 - description of the staff, p 43-44.

NAVAL INTELLIGENCE: Johnson becomes DNI (1949-1952), p 259 ff; Foreign intelligence activities, p 261-3; weekly conferences with the Navy, p 266; naval attaches, p 268; policy statements, p 268-270; Korea and intelligence, p 271; Johnson retires for health reasons on Sept. 1, 1952, p 272-3; relationship with CIA, p 273-5; relationship with the State Department, p 275; ONI runs an intelligence school, p 276-8.

NAVAL RESERVE: p 116.

Navy PUBLIC RELATIONS DIRECTOR (1946): p 217; p 223 ff; cruises for civilians, p 225-6; Congressional tours, p 227; program to "sell Navy", p 228, p 235-6; use of the J. Walter Thompson Agency, p 229-230; Combat Art, p 235; Public Information, p 235; speech writers, p 240; aided in Congressional Testimony on new Department of Defense, p 241; the Navy and Public Relations, p 242-3; Internal public relations, p 244; Johnson not very happy in this assignment, p 247-8; press relations of RADM Richard E. Byrd, p 249; question of security, p 249-250.

USS NEVADA: used as cruise ship for midshipmen, p 45.

NEWPORT, R.I.: p 256-7.

NIMITZ, Fleet Admiral Chester W.: p 159-160; p 173; p 223, 238, 242.

NUNN, RADM Ira: representative of JAG to Congressional

Committees, p 203, p 206.

USS PAUL JONES: Johnson detailed to her as executive officer, p 63, 65.

USS PEGUIN - gunboat (ex North Sea mine layer): commissioned for duty with the Asiatic Fleet, p 26; equipped with main sail at Pearl Harbor to assist with the Pacific journey, p 27; Yangtze Patrol, p 28 ff; Johnson on board the second time at beginning of 2nd tour of duty with Asiatic, p 63.

PG SCHOOL: selection of new site, p 203-206.

USS PIGEON: p 26, 28-29.

USS PITTSBURG: flagship of the Asiatic Fleet (1929) - Johnson transferred to her as Flag Lieutenant, p 66; Johnson serves for six weeks as flag secretary to Adm. Mark Bristol before Adm. McVay arrives on station, p 66, 69.

USS PRESIDENT ADAMS: troop ship - Johnson as skipper before the invasion of Bougainville, p 52-3. (attack transport): Johnson named as skipper, 1943 - takes command in Noumea, p 138-9; escort protection for troop carrying mission, p 139-140; lands troops in Empress Augusta Bay, Bougainville under enemy attack, p 145-7; Johnson makes plans to bury the dead at sea, p 148-9; Johnson relieved of command to go to staff of Cinc, S. Pac, p 150-1; p 210.

REEVES, ADM. Joseph Mason: his week-end drill off Long Beach, California, p 78-9, 83, 85-6.

RICHARDSON, Adm. J. O.: p 109-110.

USS RIZAL: Asiatic Station, p 39; Johnson, at Manila, develops many contacts with Army, p 41.

Rockefeller, John D. Jr.: story of his initial interest in the restoration of Williamsburg, Va., p 74-5.

ROOSEVELT, President F. D.: on a fishing expedition at sea in USS TUSCALOOSA, p 102-3; his illegal lobster dinner, p 104; second cruise, p 105-8.

SCOTT, RADM Norman: tells Johnson about the Spanish Yacht race, p 54.

Selection - flag rank: a wartime technique, p 213-216.

SERVICE FLEET: valuable work in the Okinawa Operation, p 193-4.

SMITH, Gen. Bedell: p 273-4.

SMOOT, VADM, Roland: anonymous letter to BuPers about Smoot and his command of the DD MONSSEN, p 230-234.

SPANAGEL, RADM Herman A.: head of the PG school at time a new site was selected, p 203-4; p 206.

SPANISH OCEAN RACE: (1928) - Lambert gives permission for Johnson to serve as navigator of the yacht ATLANTIC, p 56; details of the race as seen from the yacht, p 57-62.

USS SPRINGFIELD: new light cruiser, commanded by Johnson, p 178-180; commissioning, p 181-2; the kamikaze attack off Okinawa, p 182-3; the story of the Admiral's inspection of the crew's messing compartment, p 186; part of escort for FDR on the IOWA enroute to Yalta, p 187; damage control, p 189; Okinawa campaign, p 191 ff; p 201, p 210.

USS STEWART: Reserve Fleet DD, p 18; maintenance duty, p 22-23.

USS SUMNER: Johnson to the west coast to join the SUMNER, p 24, 26.

SUTHERLAND, Lt. Gen. R. K.: Chief of Staff to Gen. MacArthur -- his protective methods, p 161-2, 174.

USS TENNESSEE: Johnson goes to her (1933) as assistant gunnery officer, p 78 ff; athletics, p 83-4.

USS THATCHER: Johnson has duty on her for brief period to take her out of commission, p 26.

TISDALE, RADM M. S.: Commandant of Midshipmen, 1942, p 133.

USS TUSCALOOSA: Cruise ship for FDR, p 102-106.

VINSON, THE Hon, Carl: p 128, p 206; helps with ROTC, p 211.

WATSON, Major General Edwin M. (Pa): aide to FDR, p 108.

WEEMS, Capt. P. V. H.: teaches in Navigation Department at Academy (1926) - develops his system of Navigation, p 42.

WILSON, Adm. Russell: Superintendent of the Naval Academy (1941)- Johnson serves as his senior aide, p 117; details of his duties, p 117 ff; leaves Naval Academy in Dec. 1941 to become Chief of Staff to Adm. King, p 131.

YANGTZE PATROL: p 28-29 ff; escorting merchant ships, p 30-31; protection of American missionaries, p 31; protecting U. S. oil companies, p 32; protection of American consulate at Ichang, p 37-8; Johnson writes on subject for Naval Institute - invited by Capt. Baldridge to become Assistant Editor of PROCEEDINGS, p 43.

YORKTOWN MINE DEPOT: Johnson ordered there as Mining Officer, p 72 ff; duties of the Mining Officer, p 75-77.

USS YOSEMITE: Repair Ship - stationed at Newport, flagship of Commander, DD Force, p 252.

www.ingramcontent.com/pod-product-compliance
Lightning Source LLC
Chambersburg PA
CBHW082200070526
44585CB00020B/2212